FUEL YOUR SOUL, TRANSFORM YOUR BODY

FOREWORD BY
ERIC RUTH

PUBLISHED BY
SCRIPTOR PUBLISHING GROUP

TABLE OF CONTENTS

FOREWORD

by Eric Ruth

We deceive ourselves. We think change is hard. Actually, it's just the opposite. Staying put in our 'Groundhog day' existence is what's hard. Reliving the same painful experiences and thoughts every day is what hurts us, and slowly breaks us down. And we do it because of false evidence appearing real: FEAR.

We fear failure. We fear the unknown. We fear change. And the longer we live in that fear, the more it governs our life and steals our life.

I lived in the self-imposed hell of my own fear for far too long. But then I found a simple way to break free. A way you can use, too, to quickly change your life and become the person you most want to be, and have the life you deserve.

I was 26 years old. I'd done nothing of consequence my entire life, nothing I could be proud of. I had no purpose and no passion, except to try and find a way to stop my downward cycle into despair.

I was average or less in almost every way, and I knew it. I ached to achieve something, anything. Not so others would respect me, but just so I would respect myself. Because I was tired of faking it. I was tired of pretending to my family and friends and the world that I was okay. I wasn't.

I was just surviving day to day. That's it.

1

I jumped from job to job, chasing quick and easy money, which I couldn't catch. I drank too much. I was divorced and living at home with my parents. They were outwardly supportive, but I knew on the inside they were scared for me.

I didn't have a plan. I just reacted. Everything I did was driven by the emotions I experienced in the moment. My daily routine lacked structure or discipline – I did what I wanted to do, not what I needed to do to move my life forward in a productive way. I was self-aware and introspective, so I could plainly see what I was doing wrong, but I lacked the willpower to change. And that crushed my self-esteem.

Writing this now – 24 years later – is hard. It resurfaces the pain. But I have the pain to thank for where I am today. Because it was the unrelenting, self-imposed emotional pain that finally got me to do something.

I started running.

I had no money to join a gym, but I had sneakers and the streets were free. So, I ran.

I couldn't run far or fast at first. And it was hard. It hurt, physically. But emotionally, it was the greatest pain reliever I'd ever experienced. Hormones are interesting things. When you get them working for you, rather than against you, amazing changes happen.

I vividly remember sitting on the front stoop of my parent's house after a run feeling steady, strong and blessed. The kind of feeling that etches a powerful memory. The kind of feeling that kills fear, overcomes inertia and fuels change. The kind of feeling that gives us passion for life.

The less we do, the less we want to do.
The more we do, the more we want to do.

I needed some measure of control over my spiraling life. Some way to slow my fall, and hopefully reverse it. Finding a better job or a new girlfriend seemed impossible at the time. But lacing up my sneakers was something I could manage.

So I started running more and more frequently. Then doing pushups and sit-ups and pull-ups, things I could do almost anywhere, anytime. Even if I only had 10 minutes, I found a way to give myself a simple daily victory.

Every day I felt better, looked better and slept better. And because of that the fear started to disappear. I stopped sabotaging myself with alcohol, fast food and late nights. I just didn't need that stuff anymore. And I didn't want to undermine my progress.

My confidence – my belief in myself – started to grow. And that's the single most profound change of all. It's the difference maker. Because confidence gives us courage to do things we wouldn't otherwise do.

Nothing miraculous suddenly happened. I wasn't a new man overnight. But I could feel things incrementally improving, and other people noticed, too. That added more fuel to my commitment. My job performance consistently got better and I started making more money. I joined a volleyball team. I read more. I began feeling good about myself for the first time in my adult life. I was taking control.

And that's when it happened…

I started a business in my spare time out of my one-bedroom apartment. It began with a single, surprising sale of $500, and grew into a $5 million per year industry leader in less than a decade, making the Inc 500 list of fastest growing companies in America two years in a row. But even better, it allowed me to meet and serve the most incredible community of people: fitness professionals.

The best fitness professionals, like the ones in this book, change lives in the most dramatic ways. You'll see that in these amazing stories. Doctors are rightfully respected for their contribution to health and wellness. I believe, and the anecdotal evidence proves, fitness professionals are due the same respect. Because their contributions are equally profound.

People who want to lose weight and get fit naturally tend to focus on physical change - how they'll look better. What they rarely realize going in is how much almost every aspect of their lives will transform. The physical benefits of consistent exercise and supportive nutrition are significant, but the emotional changes - the growth in confidence, outlook and attitude - are nothing short of awesome.

I am living proof. And so are the folks featured in this book.

Fuel Your Soul, Transform Your Body chronicles dozens of powerful stories about real people who changed not just their bodies, but their lives, through fitness. They are far more than just physical transformation stories. They're stories of overcoming doubt and fear, and conquering personal demons. These stories are the fuel that uplifts, inspires, educates and affirms everyone who has struggled to change, and hasn't let that dream die.

Just like you need food and water to fuel your body, you need motivation, inspiration, encouragement and direction to fuel your soul, mind and spirit. This book gives it to you in small, daily doses that keep you moving forward towards your goal. Almost every person in every story tried and failed at least once before breaking through. Their stories show you how they did it, and how you can do it too.

I encourage you to read the entire book one time. Then refuel every day with one story to keep your inspiration up. If one of the fitness professionals in this book is in your area, reach out for help. Some also offer online coaching services. These are some of the very best, most caring and results-oriented professionals in the industry. Exceptional men and women dedicated to their craft, and to the people they serve.

As corny as it may sound, I can promise you this: exercise releases you from your cocoon and lets you fly. It sets you free to be the best version of you.

ABOUT ERIC RUTH

 Eric Ruth is an award winning, two-time Inc 500 business owner and referral marketing specialist. He is the author of the soon to be released book, *Local By Referral*™, the Founder of LocalByReferral.com and The Referral Challenge and the creator of Pushups for Charity™, which has raised almost $2 million for injured men and women of the Armed Services.

Eric is married to Camelia Ruth, a leading small business coach, has two beautiful and accomplished teenage daughters and two lovably strange dogs. His personal philosophy is Be, Give & Grow More™.

FROM THE BAR TO THE BARBELL

by Matt Benner

"It was February 11th, 2014. With my hands quivering in fear, I began writing a letter to my daughter, knowing that one day soon, my addiction would take my life."
- Joel R.

This is the story of one man's battle with addiction and substance abuse, and how he overcame adversity through health and fitness.

I remember it was about two weeks shy of my 54th birthday, and my morning began like every other. I got dressed, ate my breakfast, and headed off to work. I pulled in to the office, unloaded my gear, and began my day, all while nursing my headache from the night before, when I heard a knock on my door. It was my boss. He asked me if I would join him for a walk, and I knew something was up. He had begun telling me that he was aware of my addiction and the condition that I had been living in. He followed up by letting me know that I was on a 30-day paid leave of absence and could consider it severance pay if I could not "clean up" and get back to work by the end of the 30 days. The first couple of nights after speaking with my boss I felt hurt, confused and ended up hitting the bottle harder than ever, but what I did next saved my life.

Growing up I was always a good student, and stayed out of trouble. I grew up a farm kid in rural Minnesota, and was the runt of the litter. For the most part I was a happy kid, except for the fact that I was labeled the "little guy." Because of my size, I tended to avoid the more physical games and sports. That ended in the 9th grade when my best friend, Mark, convinced me to join our high school wrestling team. This would not be the only influence, good or bad, that Mark had on me.

My first year of wrestling I weighed in at a whopping 77 pounds! Throughout my first wrestling season I was always competing against guys who were much bigger than I was, and I always thought of this as a good thing because it made me work twice as hard. Fast forward to the end of my wrestling career. Although still small, I was wrestling, and beating, guys that were 20, 30, and 40 pounds heavier than I was in wrestle-offs for the varsity spots. Due to an unfortunate case of mononucleosis, I missed most of my senior year, but I came back and finished the season strong, missing the state tournament by one point. I will never forget that loss, but nevertheless, I left high school filled with confidence and feeling free to roam the world without fear.

I kept growing after high school and leveled out at about 5'9" and 195 for the beginning of my young adult life. Shortly after graduating I went on to wed my high school sweetheart, a marriage that was wallowing in pity and found myself looking for something new and exciting in my life. Then in the winter of 1984-1985, my good friend, Mark, re-entered my life.

Mark offered me a job working in a gold mine in Alaska, and I jumped at it, thinking this was just the adventure that I needed. Upon my arrival, I could not have been more excited to be thousands of miles from where I grew up, with one of my childhood best friends. We spent the first couple of days bar hopping around town, and I was really enjoying myself. One evening at the bar, I noticed that Mark and my new friends (his current friends) were making an unusual number of trips to the bathroom, and at the time, I didn't think too much of it. Shortly afterward I found out why. Keep in mind I was just a farm kid from the Midwest, and had not known much about what went on in the world. Mark and his friends were far deeper into alcohol than I knew, and were heavy into using cocaine, and pot, and it scared me to death. The only other person I knew was Mark's uncle, and he lived in Anchorage, which was roughly 5 hours away and a massive snow storm had just arrived in town. However, as nervous as I was, I was more scared to stay in that environment, so I packed up my truck, and made the drive to Anchorage.

I arrived in Anchorage, and in the Spring, I found work at a paint store. This is where I settled down, and began feeling stable for the first time in a long time. I purchased a gym membership, and began working out regularly, joined a softball team, and picked up my golf. It was a strange game to pick-up in Alaska, but I was hooked. Shortly after, I rekindled an old flame, and we ended up getting married, and started a family together with the birth of my girl. Life was great, and things were finally going my way. I was working out regularly, had a great relationship, and had even gotten myself a bigger job as an outside salesman.

Little did I know that my job as a salesman came with large amounts of pressure, and after trying to relax, the only way I found to cope was the effect of alcohol. When I was drinking, I could shut everything out, and it relieved me from the stress that I was feeling. My coping mechanism continued, and eventually turned into an addiction. The substance abuse took over my life outside of work, and eventually contributed to the destruction of my marriage. We divorced in 1994 and both left Alaska. My ex-wife and daughter, Zoee, moved to Texas, and I went to California. I moved around a lot and finally landed in Spokane, WA in December of 2000. I had a new girlfriend by then, and we shared the same hobbies. We drank and smoked up a storm and our diet plan consisted mostly of meat, potatoes, and booze. By the time I was in my mid-40's, I was tipping the scales at 240 pounds and my blood pressure was through the roof. My fitness was out the window. I was also diagnosed with a sleeping disorder called (Alpha Intrusions) which does not let your brain "turn off" long enough to go into REM sleep. My Doctor put me on a diet and exercise plan consisting of lots of salads, little to no booze or smoking, biking, walking and some light calisthenics. I got down to around 190 lbs. All's well, right?

Then my now 17-year old daughter, Zoee, re-entered my life with a vengeance. She was pregnant and not unlike her father, she had her own struggles with substance abuse. Once again, my "Midwestern Values" led me to encourage her to have the baby, and I happily welcomed my first grandchild - a boy she named Keegan.

Unfortunately, things did not go well for either my daughter or myself. She succumbed to Heroin addiction, and I fell into a deep depression and extremely heavy drinking and left my girlfriend over it all. By now I was tipping the scales at over 250 pounds and back to massive stress, anxiety, and high blood pressure. It was so bad I even gave up on golf. It was at this time in my life that I bring you back to the moment that my boss had confronted me. After nights of heavy drinking, my daughter finally persuaded me to take up my boss' offer, and I did. I followed his instruction, and entered detox, followed by an intensive outpatient program or (IOP). I made it back to work on the 28th day.

During my time at IOP I heard of a place called Pura Vida Recovery, which is a not-for-profit organization dedicated to helping people in recovery get back on their feet through what they call Mind, Body, and Spirit support. I frequented Pura Vida and met some wonderful people who were going through their own similar troubles. I did some yoga and attended a few meetings but the physical portion of their program was beyond my limited abilities at the time. After consulting my doctor, I began physical therapy because at this point I was having difficulty even walking around.

My therapy went well and, when completed, my therapist recommended Complete Athlete (CA) as my next step in getting my health back. I joined immediately and was determined that I would never look back. I wanted to live the way God intended for me to live - healthy and sober.

This is where my real fitness story begins and continues. I weighed in around the second week of January 2017 at an untidy 242 pounds with my first personal trainer, Jon. He helped me learn the proper ways to move and exercise so I could do more good than harm (it turns out most of what I had done in my former life was at least somewhat incorrect). As part of my CA membership I was introduced to Jolene, a nutritionist, who set me up with an app called My Fitness Pal. It helps me track my nutrition to the letter, and she also set me up on an Isogenix plan to enhance my weight loss.

I currently work out 3 days a week with a small group led by my trainer, Matt. Combining the work-outs with Matt and the proper nutrition plan from Jolene, I now weigh about 217 pounds as of this writing. That means I have lost 25 pounds in a little over two months, and continue getting better every single day. I also consult with Mike, the sports chiropractor at CA, and he is helping me, physically, so I can work better with my golf instructor. Getting my game back in shape is one of my first priorities.

I feel better now, at 54 years of age, then I did at 44. I have tons of energy and sleep better than I ever have. I am looking forward to the summer and re-embracing my golf game with vigor. If I lose a few more pounds, I might even use my pool. I always look forward to my workouts with my friends at Complete Athlete and will continue to keep coming back as long as they will have me.

ABOUT MATT BENNER

Matt Benner is a Client Care Specialist for Complete Athlete. He is a native of Spokane, WA and was a collegiate athlete playing baseball for the Vikings at Big Bend C.C. and the Yellowjackets at Montana State University.

Matt enjoys spending time in the outdoors, running, hiking and fishing, and is currently preparing for his first Ironman Triathlon!

BELIEVE ME, YOU CAN DO THIS!

by Marcus Brugger

My name is Marcus Brugger, and I grew up in an over-weight family. I never understood how everyone in my family could be over-weight except me. Eventually, I realized what made us different. Spoiler alert: No, I wasn't the mailman's son. I had totally different habits. I was the most active, and I had a healthy relationship with food. I ate for nourishment and not comfort or out of boredom.

After understanding our differences, I decided to become a weight loss coach. For the last 13 years, I have helped many people lose 125+ pounds all the way down to their pesky last 10 pounds! Five years ago, I opened Movement Fitness and set out to create a supportive and inspiring culture that helped people lose weight without dieting. Along the way, we have helped many people lose weight, feel and look better. We not only changed their bodies, but also their minds.

Two years ago, I met what I thought was an ordinary woman who just needed a good push, but it turns out I was dead wrong. She was more than an ordinary person. She was an exceptional person who just needed a little help to get past her weight loss beliefs. Little did I know her story would also have a huge impact on me and many others. Below is her story told through my eyes.

Door #1 - 2 Feet to the Right

As I sit there waiting for a first-time client to walk in the door, I am reviewing her information. She is a 42-year old woman, 50-pounds over-weight and sedentary for the past 2 years. The minutes tick by past 10:30 am and there is no sight of her. Just as I am about to write her off, slowly the door opens and a timid woman quickly walks in, opening the door just enough to scurry through. Her name was Kristi. She seemed very uneasy and unsure of walking in, as if she had a foot out the door, ready to bolt.

It was 10 minutes past our appointment time. What I didn't know was Kristi was actually not only on time but early. See had been sitting in her car for the last 15 minutes. You see, there is another gym directly next to us, literally 2 feet between the two doors. Kristi wasn't sure which door to go in.

Even worse, Kristi saw the type of women that were walking out of the other gym next door; skinny, and the type of women who have never been an ounce overweight, in her mind. As Kristi sat there watching each woman exit their workout session with a Starbucks Grande Caramel Macchiato, she started to panic. She thought, "This can't be right!" She immediately called her husband and told him, "I just can't go through with it, there are nothing but Barbie bitches coming out with lattes!" He spent the next 5 minutes talking her off the ledge and simply stated, why don't you just try door #1 if you don't think door #2 is the right place for you?

Leap of Faith #1

This seemingly small event was actually the first monumental step Kristi took to change her life. She could have mentally justified driving away and never looked back. Instead, she demonstrated courage and took her first leap of faith by opening our door.

Kristi walked in, wondering if she was in the right place and ready to bolt like a gazelle being chased by a lion in the African Safari. I welcomed her with a smile and a firm but tender hand shake. She immediately asked, "Is this Movement Fitness?" I replied with "Yes, you are in the right place, and don't worry, we aren't associated with the gym next door!"

Before I even finished my sentence, I saw Kristi's body language relax, and suddenly she let down the defensive wall that had been forcefully constructed before she walked in.

Over the next hour I got to know Kristi. I learned:

What kind of a person she is.

How she moved.

What she would need help with.

And her weight loss beliefs.

Leap of Faith #2

After the 60-minute assessment, it was like a switch went off. Kristi was a totally different person. She went from a state of fight or flight, to smiling, excited and ready to take her second leap of faith. Kristi eagerly signed up for a 1 year membership and practically skipped out of the studio with a huge smile on her face as if she just won the lottery!

As the months rolled by Kristi was committed as ever. She never missed a session and gave it everything she had in the workouts. The only problem was Kristi had one BIG issue, and that was her weight loss beliefs. "I can't eat carbs or I will gain weight and be fat!" On top of that she was a firm believer that if she simply just didn't eat, then she would drop the pounds.

Leap of Faith #3

Kristi became more and more frustrated with her results. At this point, she had only lost 3 pounds in 3 months. She came to me and said, "I just don't get this. I am working out harder than I have ever worked out in my life and I have ONLY LOST 3 POUNDS IN 3 MONTHS!" After listening to her frustration, I used this opportunity to reinforce the education Kristi had been so resistant to follow. I explained the value and long-term benefits of eating carbs and more food. At this point, Kristi was learning that her own beliefs were holding her back and was ready to open her mind to change these beliefs and put different behavior into action. This was a huge leap of faith when she started eating more carbohydrates and the correct amount of calories!

Kristi ate more than she ever thought she could. She was full, had more energy, and her weight dropped immediately. In the next month, she lost 15 pounds! Five times what she lost in the prior 3 months combined!

Month after month, Kristi ate more and lost more. Slowly but surely, she hit her goal and then some. In 10 months Kristi lost 57 pounds, 10% body fat and 40 inches!

How did all of this happen???

Kristi changed her weight loss beliefs!

Yes, believe it or not, you have **weight loss beliefs!** They are how you view yourself losing weight or getting the body you always wanted, or used to have.

Now, YOU have positive weight loss beliefs and negative ones. The problem is the negative beliefs are the ones that keep you from getting to your goals.

These are conscious and subconscious thoughts that turn into beliefs and result in YOUR actions.

They are created by fear, control, expectations, and time frames. These are road bumps that make you drift off your path to success if YOU don't see things going your perfect way.

Let's be honest here. Ever wonder why all of a sudden you go from doing perfectly to just giving up or suddenly falling off?

It's YOUR weight loss thoughts that control your weight loss beliefs and result in your weight loss ACTIONS!

The secret is that you can actually control this by using your thoughts.

3 Things YOU can do to Change:

1. **Know YOU are enough!**

   You have what it takes. Anything else is simply untrue!

2. **Realize it is possible!**

   Give everything YOU have into it and see what happens!

3. **No Matter What, Keep Going!**

   This is mindset that will change everything!

BONUS: CHANGE YOUR WEIGHT LOSS THOUGHTS FROM NEGATIVE TO POSITIVE!

Whenever you catch yourself saying, "That's not possible!" or "I can't do this," correct the negative phrase with a positive phrase. Choose a positive mantra phrase that you can say that will replace that negative.

Here's mine: Believe Me, YOU Can Do This!

What's YOURS? _____

Want to take it further??

Send me your positive mantra phrase. marcusbrugger@gmail.com

Take the time to FOCUS on the steps and it will feel like a miracle when everything starts to fall into place, and you hit your weight loss goals once and for all!

About Marcus Brugger

My name is Marcus Brugger. For the last 12 years I have helped busy professionals lose weight and look and feel better. I have worked with clients of all different backgrounds- from experienced, to inexperienced, from clients who have tried it all and failed, to clients who don't know where to start.

My passion is helping clients achieve goals they never thought were possible. Every day I am driven to not only help each client but also to make a positive life changing difference.

Your Body Never Works Against You

By Jenny May Clermont

I used to train for physique competitions, and in order for me to get lean enough to place in the top 3, I had to be very regulated with my foods. In addition, I would try to keep my estrogen levels very low on top of a hefty training schedule. After all, as a woman, it is those higher estrogen levels that cause women to have a higher percent body fat than men.

At the time I was a chemist, working and creating hormone replacement products in the pharmaceutical industry. One of the many reasons women often consider hormone replacement products is because of the weight gain and fat storage shift to the midsection (or muffin top). The hope is that these products will help them lose the muffin top and extra weight.

Now as a female physique competitor you can imagine my curiosity as to what was happening, hormonally, to cause menopausal women who were losing estrogen to gain weight – when I was working to keep my estrogen levels low to lose weight.

It turns out that it is not that simple.

There are a whole host of changes that happen, the state of adrenal fatigue a woman is in as she enters peri-menopause, frequently determines how much and how fast she'll gain weight. Believe it or not, your fat cells become part of your endocrine system and help convert one hormone to another so you can keep functioning.

If there is one thing I have learned over the last 13 years that I have been working in the fitness industry, plus the 15 as a chemist, it is that your body never works against you. It does the very best it can with what we give it.

What most folks don't realize is that you can, and will, literally, change your chemistry and hormonal balance when you change your nutritional intake and your training style. Your nutrition and mode of exercise directly impacts your hormone profile. It is awesome that you can make those sorts of changes with just minor adjustments.

For example, let's take Sally (not her real name). Sally was in her 40's, worked out 5 days a week and wanted to lose 5 pounds. Unfortunately, she was gaining weight and she also had a lot of stress in her life. When I met Sally she was eating 1000 calories a day and looking to add two more days of training to her hectic life and training schedule. I assured her doing more and eating less would only lead to more belly fat as a result of her exhausted adrenals. Sally didn't like what I had to say, she was hooked on the release she got from working out and running, so the idea of doing less horrified her.

My prescription for Sally was 4 days of weight training, not body pump, not HIIT, not metabolic, or weight loss circuits, but traditional strength training – and if she was to do anymore, it would have to be in the form of yoga or walking. The strength training and yoga were modes of exercise that would lower her cortisol levels and give her adrenals a break. Plus, she stopped focusing on calories and started to focus on getting enough macro-nutrients to fuel her metabolism. You know what happened? Those 5 pounds fell off her within a couple of weeks.

Your body is complicated. It creates something like 400 billion chemical reactions every second to keep you functioning, alive and well. From what I've seen most people start an exercise and/or nutrition program that often works against their bodies' needs. Maybe their friends are doing it, or they saw it on TV, or whatever, without any real consideration for what their body actually needs. Everybody is different and has unique needs, so knowing specifically where to start is key and may truly make the difference between success and failure.

The other part of the equation is understanding any habits, beliefs or associations you have that may be preventing you from experiencing real success. The lack of awareness around these limiting beliefs is really what prevents people from achieving true success. Over the last few years, helping people work through these limiting beliefs has become a larger part of what we do.

The combination of creating awareness of any self-limiting beliefs related to emotional eating, education of what your body needs and how your choices impact your body and your hormones is key to improving your choices on a consistent basis. The more you learn and understand how things like alcohol and sugar create hormonal chaos, the more empowered you are to correct hormonal balance and enable change by making better choices more frequently. Ultimately that is my mission - to get you started on the best path to achieve your goals. I want to educate you every step of the way so your body gets what it needs, and you get results so you can live life to the fullest potential.

ABOUT JENNY MAY CLERMONT

Jenny May walked away from a successful 15-year career as a pharmaceutical chemist (most of which revolved around women's hormone therapy products) to pursue her lifelong passion and dream... to help women (and men) reclaim their figures, their health and their lives... NATURALLY!

Jenny May has over 25 years of research on diet and exercise with the purpose of gaining a deeper understanding in regard to how diet and exercise affects your hormone profile, performance and body fat levels. She is the author of Menopausal Fitness & You and has successfully coached hundreds of women around the Globe to reclaim their lives & their bodies during the menopausal years.

Fitness is not just a job for Jenny May, it is a passion; one that she lives and breathes every day. Her goal is to educate & empower you on how to use whole foods & exercise to create hormonal balance to live a more healthy and active lifestyle once and for all.

Contact: jennymayclermont@gmail.com

THREE CASE STUDIES RAISE AN INTERESTING QUESTION:

WHAT MOTIVATES YOU TO WORKOUT, FEAR OR LOVE?

by Aaron Crocker

Case Study #1: Erica*

One sunny day Erica is enjoying the vibrant life deserving any 27-year-old single woman.

The following day she's told by her doctor she has cancer. The shock of the news is matched only by the diagnosis to follow: Stage 3 breast cancer. In a matter of moments, she learns the aggressive, nine-centimeter cancerous lump has already spread to eight of her lymph nodes.

She never knew life could be shrouded in such darkness while the sun shone so brightly. Facing her grim diagnosis, she's forced to confront the unthinkable…

Case Study #2: Tina*

Desperate to solve her lifelong weight problem, Tina schemed up a dangerous plan to finally shed the weight, hopefully for good.

Previously, she had applied for Lap-Band(R) surgery but was shocked to discover she was eight pounds under the required weight to qualify for the risky procedure. It was the first time in her life she was ever considered underweight for anything, and it couldn't have been worse news.

Devastated, she decided to do the unimaginable; she committed to gaining eight more pounds of fat to qualify for the invasive surgery…

Case Study #3: Richard*

The doctor entered the room and cleared his throat.

Using a tone more akin a pastor than a physician, he looked at Richard and said, "…Your blood is not even red anymore; it's pink from all the fat mixed in with it. If you don't start exercising and eating right, you're not going to live very long. You understand what I'm saying, right?"

What the doctor said next made Richard realized his blood was so rancid, Dracula wouldn't drink it…

Don't worry; I won't leave you hanging. In just a moment, I'll come back and finish telling you the rest of these stories.

But before I do, I hope you'll pause for just a moment to consider something important.

If you had to guess, what would you say is the primary motivation behind each of these case studies? In other words, what do you think drove their decisions to start an exercise program?

The question is worth asking because it deals with something important to the human condition.

Identity.

Identity in the sense of what's internally motivating a person too start exercising: fear or love.

While both fear and love are highly effective motivators, when it comes to you, dear reader, it's my highest hope you'll choose love before fear becomes your primary motivation.

When love is your motivation, you'll come to realize something valuable: getting in shape is not only about restoring your health; it's about redeeming every area of your life.

But when fear is your primary reason for getting in shape, you're probably motivated by survival.

I say that because if a man decides to lose weight only after his wife leaves him, he's operating in fear.

Fear he's not sufficient. Fear no one else will love him the way he is. Fear he's no longer as attractive as he once was, reducing his chances in a highly competitive dating world.

Particularly in the case of marital breakups, fear has a nasty way of turning into a worse emotion: revenge.

Revenge weight loss is typical in our industry. "I'll make you sorry you left me!" Some version of that sentiment is worth untold millions of dollars to the fitness industry.

It's a shame, really, and it's not the motivation the trainers in this book want for you. We'd all prefer you operating on a much higher and wholesome level of emotional reasoning.

We'd all much rather you understand something important about yourself:

YOU ARE WHAT YOU LOVE

If the language of love sounds to froufrou for your taste, then feel free to change the word love to desire. You'll still get there.

We are what we love. Our wants, longings, and desires are at the core of our identity, the motivating reason behind our actions and behavior.

If we can agree on such a premise, then we can conclude another important truth: You need to know what motivates you. You need to know what you want. You need to know what you desire.

You need to know what you love. You need to know what you fear.

If, after taking a close look at your motives, you discover fear is your primary motivator for getting in shape, well, let's just be honest about it. If fear is what it takes to get you exercising, you might as well use it to change your life!

Because (and this is especially true if you are working with a professional trainer) one day soon you'll find yourself working out for higher, more wholesome reasons. Like a genuine sense of personal satisfaction and accomplishment with your results.

Until then, let me ask again: What do you want?

In your consideration of the question, try not to make an intellectual exercise out of it. I want just the opposite for you, in fact. I don't want you to answer the question from the calm, cool, and collected areas of your logical, analytical brain. For our purpose, that would be a mistake.

Answer from the deepest, most personal desires found in the center of your gut. Feel your answers, don't think your answers. I want you to know what you want in your gut.

Why is this important? Because once you "feel" your answers, you can effectively wrap your intellect around them. When you know in your heart of hearts the reasons why you want to get in shape, your logical brain quickly catches up.

When that happens, going to the gym is easy! It's when you try to logically persuade yourself you need to workout that makes going to the gym a drudgery.

But, what if you hate to exercise? How do you ever motivate yourself to start an exercise program?

Well, there are two ways:

1) Like the three stories that opened this chapter, you can have an unfortunate inciting event; a catalyst that forces you to take action. There may be nothing more powerful than a doctor's negative prognoses to kickstart your survival instinct. Like Erica, who received a cancer diagnosis. Or like Richard, whose blood had so much fat in it, the color turned pink.

2) You can change your mind. You possess that magical power! I used to hate doing barbell squats with a passion. Refused to do them. I made every excuse under the sun. But then, one day I decided to change my mind. I said to myself, "I'll learn to love doing squats!" I meant it, I set my heart to it, and I practiced, practiced, practiced until it worked. That was 35 years ago, and to this day, squats are still my favorite exercise.

For that reason, and many others, I can tell you from personal experience operating from a motivation of love for exercise (translatable to all areas of your life) is a lot more fulfilling than reacting from fear.

When you know what you love and start working from that premise, you'll start seeing results you thought were out of your reach. You'll handle problems outside the gym that would normally stress you out. And you'll solve personal problems you expected to carry for the rest of your life.

Now, as promised, let's get back to the case studies that opened this chapter.

Case Study #1: Erica

For most of us, there's nothing more horrifying than the fear of a cancer diagnosis. For 27 year old Erica, it came as a total shock. As you can probably imagine, the aggressive surgery, combined with 5-months of chemotherapy and radiation treatments stripped her of her hair, took a beating on her body and robbed her of her self-confidence. The steroids wouldn't let her sleep, causing her to gain a lot of weight.

But Erica wasn't ready to give up on life and knew she needed to remain confident about the future. So, as soon as she could, she joined a gym offering supervised group classes. And the results are nothing less than spectacular!

"I remember the day I saw people doing pull ups, and I said to myself, "That's impossible. I could never do that." Today, I'm thrilled to say I do the impossible! Working out has given me back the confidence cancer stole from me. Cancer put me on my back; working out put me back on my feet. Now, I'm in nursing school because I want to help other cancer patients."

Case Study #2: Tina

After deliberately gaining an additional eight pounds (now at her heaviest bodyweight ever) to qualify for Lap-Band surgery, her insurance provider denied her request to pay for the procedure. So, instead of a surgeon's scalpel cutting her open, she found a gym determined to help her.

In her first week of training, she lost 9.5 pounds. In only 28 days she dropped 23 pounds and is so thankful she didn't undergo that drastic, life-threatening procedure.

Case Study #3: Richard

I don't know how you'd feel if your doctor told you, "Your blood is not even red anymore; it's pink from all the fat mixed in with it…" But I can tell you how Richard felt. He feared he was going to die decades before his time.

And for a good reason too, because according to his doctor, his triglyceride levels were off the chart. Normal triglyceride levels should be under 150. Borderline is 150-199. High is 200-499. Very high is 500 or more. Richard's triglyceride level was 2,000! In other words, his blood was so thick with fat, the extra pressure against his veins was so great, it was making his normal blood pressure horror blood pressure!

Not only that, he was a Type 2 diabetic, taking seven pills a day to manage his disease. But now, after working with caring fitness professionals, what was once a clogged artery system flows freely again. The proof came when he returned to see his doctor a few months later, and the change in his blood work was so drastic it shocked his doctor!

"I don't know what you're doing, but keep it up! Your triglycerides have plummeted from 2,000 to 132! Congratulations, you are no longer a diabetic, and you can stop taking your medication!"

There you have it; three testimonies, transformations, indeed, transfigurations of core identities from fear to love.

A heavy question to consider, however, is this: Was all this fear-based motivation necessary to get these same results?

Hypothetically speaking, what if, just for the love of exercise, Erica, Tina, and Richard had been working out long before the inciting incidents fearfully forced them to act?

Would, could, love of exercising have staved off the diseases that almost cost Erica and Richard their lives? What if, Tina had committed to loving exercising long before she gained so much weight that she was ready to undergo the risky Lap-Band(R) surgery?

What if, dear reader, you start cultivating and curating your heart to love exercise and eating right? What if love had the power to change your life before tragedy strikes?

It's what I hope for you. I hope you'll find the love of life, of family, of faith, and yes, of yourself, has the power to break the logjam of a sedentary lifestyle.

To get started, you may have to exercise something else before you start exercising your body. You may have to exercise your faith. Faith, rooted in God's gift of volition, giving you the ability to change your mind, like I did with squats.

A faith rooted in the conviction that, sometimes, we have to do things before we know things. A life-changing truth that proves we must change our hearts before we can transform our bodies.

Our attitudes have to change, our minds have to change, and our hearts have to change.

So, I'll say it again. You have the power to change your mind. You possess the power to change your attitude from one of, "I hate to exercise," to "I love to exercise."

With such power at your disposal, you have a decision to make today. Out of love, I hope you'll decide to set your heart on loving exercise and good nutrition.

Here's how to find a trainer to help you get started:

1) Look to see if one of the authors of this book is in your city. If so, consider yourself blessed and contact her or him.

2) If none of these authors are in your city, then go to https://www. acefitness.org/acefit/locate-trainer/ and type in your zip code. It'll bring up all the personal trainers in your area.

3) Or you can put the word out to your sphere of influence on Facebook, and ask your friends for recommendations. Just make sure the trainer of your choice is certified and insured.

4) Follow through.

*Note: The names in this article have been changed to protect the privacy of the individuals, but the stories are true.

ABOUT AARON CROCKER

Aaron Crocker is considered by experts in the field as one of the fitness industry's leading copywriting, advertising, and marketing strategists.

He had the honor of serving as the marketing and advertising implementer behind Birmingham's own Iron Tribe Fitness. His marketing strategies contributed to Iron Tribe's swift rise from a garage gym hobby to one of the fastest growing franchise gyms in the world.

He helped pioneer and open the first Fitness Together franchise in the Southeast with his good friend, Forrest Walden. Together, they grew the franchise to twelve locations with seventy-two employees in only three years.

On a local level, Aaron has been featured in Birmingham Magazine, Birmingham Business Journal, and Over the Mountain Journal. He's been interviewed by Fox 6 News and featured on both Good Morning Alabama, as well, as being a regular guest on Exercise Monday Morning. Nationally, he's been featured in Personal Fitness Professional magazine.

He was awarded the Personal Trainer of The Year in 2003. The Fitness Together franchise units Aaron and Forrest co-owned were awarded the Franchise of The Year twice, and Franchise of The Month on eleven different occasions.

Above his professional career, the most important aspects of Aaron's life are his faith, wife of thirty-seven years, and two children, who have gifted him with eight grandchildren.

You can reach him at 2aaroncrocker@gmail.com

Confessions of a Former Sugar Addict

by Anna Dornier

October 10, 2016, 2:36 am. I was jolted awake by a shooting pain on my right knee. No matter which position I switched to, the pain wouldn't go away. I got up to go to the bathroom, and I winced at the pain of bending my knees. I had to hold on to the walls just to minimize the pain. At first I thought this was an old injury resurfacing. I had pulled a ligament a couple of years ago when I used my right leg to prevent falling off the stairs while I was carrying my 1-year old son, Lucas. However, on this day, the pain was becoming stronger and stronger, and I could no longer ignore it.

Just 4 days prior, I gave birth to our daughter and 2nd child, Isabella. The pain started at just a bit over annoying level towards the end of my 2nd pregnancy. I knew it was there, but I thought to myself that it's probably due to the extra weight I'm carrying and that it's most likely going to go away after I give birth. Well, I was so wrong because it just kept getting worse. The truth is, I was in denial. I didn't want to think that I was developing arthritis. I mean, I'm 34 years old, and I'm a fitness trainer. I pride myself in eating well and staying active, and I coach clients every day to do the same!

On top of the pain, the stress of taking care of our newborn full-time, along with sleep deprivation and managing multiple businesses at the same time, was starting to take a toll on me... and my appetite. I've always known that stress can trigger hunger hormones but this was no ordinary hunger. My husband always joked that I eat like a teenage boy who plays football, and I don't deny the fact that I have always had a huge appetite. But, this was different. I have always eaten my 5-6 meals a day religiously, but this time my hunger came back with a vengeance after only 20 minutes of eating my last meal! The fact that I was breastfeeding probably didn't help either and when I did wake up in the middle of the night to feed Isabella, my hunger would be so unbearable that I had to eat high-carb foods like our kids' cereal or frozen waffles, instant mac and cheese from the pantry, etc. just to fall back asleep!

These late-night carb binges became such a nightmare during the day because it led to me craving carbs and sugar all the time. I drank 5 cups of coffee a day to fool myself into believing that I needed the caffeine to help me with my sleep deprivation, but it really was a way for me to satisfy my sweet tooth that was getting out of hand. I thought I was done with my sweet tooth! I grew up with my Mom, drinking Coke for breakfast and pretty much every meal she ate. We would have dessert after dinner every night and whenever we went out to eat! That was me, before my fitness coaching days. The first thing I looked at was the dessert menu whenever I would sit down to place my order at a restaurant. This was one of the reasons I loved working in the fitness industry because working with clients on helping them make healthy lifestyle choices kept me accountable to my own. Now, I was back to being a sugar-addict.

"Hi, my name is Anna Dornier, and I am a sugar-addict." Truly, that was going through my head all the time. This can't be happening! At this point, my left thumb started to hurt to the point where gripping anything, let alone pull my pants up with my left hand, was excruciating.

I have got to do something about this. I was falling apart! When I sat down in a group of older people talking about the ailments they were having, the pain they were experiencing, and the gobs of medications they were taking, it all echoed in my head. Is it true that as we get old, we start to fall apart? But, I'm only 34 years old! If a 34-year old, active woman, like me, who eats fairly healthy can have all these issues, what hope is there for other people who aren't making healthy lifestyle choices?

Most of all, I was scared of developing diabetes. My Mom and 2 older brothers both have it and their blood glucose is still not within normal range even with the multiple types of insulin they are taking. Diabetes runs rampant for the rest of both sides of my family as well. To be truthful, I am in the career that I am in because I not only do not want that be my fate, I also want to let other people know that being genetically predisposed to it does not necessarily mean that they will have it. Diabetes can be controlled through our lifestyle choices, or can it? The fact that I developed gestational diabetes during my 2nd pregnancy was gnawing at my insides. What if that was the start of me truly developing this disease? I tried to console myself saying that that's different because pregnancy hormones affect our blood sugar metabolism. That is true, but it still did not change the fact that I was having all this pain, and I had a feeling that somehow my sugar-addiction is causing it.

I finally reached a breaking point. I had to ask for professional help, other than my own. I had already decided that I wanted to do a fitness bikini competition after my pregnancy. I've always wanted to do it just so I can check it off of my bucket list, and I figured the best way to do it was after I am completely done making babies which is, well, now. I found an online coach to keep me accountable and possibly help me deal with my sugar-addiction. She had me doing what she called the Fat

Adapted meal plan. I questioned everything about it because it wasn't the type of meal plan I expected to get. She had me eating lower protein, higher fat meals with a ton of salt! I had bacon, avocado, sausages, whole eggs as part of my meals. Well, either she was out of her mind or she really knew what she was doing. My thought was, "Well, what I am doing is clearly not working for me, so I might as well try her way."

To my surprise, the pain on my right knee and my left thumb started to subside day after day. After 3 months of being on the Fat Adapted meal plan, I was completely pain free. My hunger and sugar addiction was still there but it wasn't as intense. I was still sleep-deprived, something I can't help by having a newborn, but I wasn't as tired during the day. I gained 46 lbs during my pregnancy and I lost 49 lbs after 4 months of being on this plan which means that I have returned to my pre-pregnancy shape. I actually weigh even less now than before I got pregnant. My results propelled me to investigate the Fat Adapted meal plan further because the fitness coach in me had to find out why and how this simple switch has made such a tremendous difference to my health and vitality.

I found out from my research that Fat Adapted is another name for the Ketogenic diet. This definitely was not the first time I've heard of this diet but I never really taken the time to do my research on it. I assumed it was some fad diet that didn't work and wasn't realistic for me or my clients. I was so completely and utterly wrong. I spent the next few months reading every book and scientific research I can get my hands on the Ketogenic ("keto") diet. At first, it was all for my own knowledge and benefit. I wanted to understand why I experienced the results that I had. I also wanted to find out if there were other people experiencing similar results. The more I dove into the subject, the more I liked what I was learning. I found that ketosis is a state where your body burns your stored body fat for fuel when you lower your carbohydrate and protein intake long enough. By eating this way, I was able to switch my body into burning fat for fuel (fat is converted into ketones in our liver - it is an energy source that our bodies can use besides glucose) instead of relying on carbs as my main energy source. When I eliminated my need for carbs as my main source of fuel, I also eliminated having to manage the ups and downs of my blood glucose which is the case when I ate carbs. Basically, switching to becoming a fat-burner instead of a carb-burner, helped eliminate any inflammation I had. This also explains why I am now completely pain-free.

While my appetite has been back to normal, my sugar cravings still nagged at me daily. I was still obsessing about making keto-friendly desserts just so I could satisfy my sweet tooth. I thought to myself that maybe I'm just doomed to deal with my sugar addiction for the rest of my life. I thought that maybe this was the one struggle I couldn't overcome and I thought that it was ironic because I am, after all, a fitness coach. I started to think that maybe I just like to sabotage myself. My sugar-addiction, literally and figuratively, kept me from becoming the best version of myself. As a believer in God and His power, I refused to give-in to the devil's temptations. But, the more I gave into my sugar craving urges, the more I was not able to undertake God's mission for my life. I wasn't about to let that happen. Not in this lifetime.

Eight months into living the ketogenic lifestyle, I had a call from a former client of mine out of the blue. He mentioned that his friend's niece, Mykle, was telling him about an exogenous ketone drink that claimed to put anyone in ketosis an hour after taking the drink. He knew I was doing the diet part so he thought I might be interested in hearing what she had to say. I was skeptical but since I'm deep into my research on ketosis, I was willing to hear Mykle out. I grilled her with questions and the more she answered, the more I got intrigued. She mentioned the company uses Dr. Dominic D'Agostino's formula and he happens to be the pioneer in ketones and ketosis research. That was the credibility I needed to at least give it a try.

My first experience with the supplement was nothing short of amazing. I took it an hour before I worked out and I had this surge in energy like no other. I sprinted at 10 miles per hour and I felt like I was jogging and my feet were so light! I also deadlifted 40 lbs heavier than I normally would which meant I hit a new personal record. I went straight to my computer and started working. I had such mental clarity and focus for the next 4 hours or so that I didn't even realize that I didn't think about food or sugar during that time. Needless to say, Mykle got a thank you call from me that day and I also jokingly asked her if this stuff was legal.

The combination of living the ketogenic lifestyle and taking exogenous ketones has been such a powerful combination that not only helped me overcome my sugar-addiction, it is also helping me become better in other areas of my life. I didn't realize how much my obsession to sugar controlled my life until it was completely gone. Today, I eat 1-2 times a day and I'm fully satisfied eating high-fat foods like bacon, cheese, avocados, heavy cream, grass-fed butter, all-natural sausages and deli meats, just to name a few of my favorites. I'm also happy to report that after a year of living this lifestyle, my blood work came back and my Triglycerides went from a high normal of 170 mg/dL down to 65 mg/dL and my bad cholesterol went from normal down to the low range. I also started recommending the supplement to my Mom and 2 brothers who went from their usual high blood glucose ranges of 300-200 mg/dL down to the normal range of 99 and below.

Since starting my journey to becoming Fat Adapted back in October 2015, I have been able to coach hundreds of clients make the switch to using ketones for energy either through the meal plans, the supplement or a combination of both. While I'm not firmly convinced that the ketogenic diet is for everyone, I urge everyone I meet to at least try it so they can assess for themselves what works best for them based on their results and experience. If anything, adding the exogenous supplement to their current meal plan can give them the benefits of ketosis without actually living a fully ketogenic lifestyle.

I couldn't imagine where my life would be without ketones fueling my body. As always, God came through for me and he helped me find a solution to what seemed like a problem that would forever have a strong grip on me. As a result, I am able to be a better warrior for His kingdom, a better wife, a better Mom, and a better fitness coach. I know my journey has just begun, and I am excited for all the people that are bound to find their way into this way of life. As I continue my own journey, I will always, "Walk by faith, not by sight," 2 Corinthians 5:7.

ABOUT ANNA DORNIER

Anna is the founder and owner of Transform FX Fitness Transformation Centers. She fell in love with pumping iron, how it made her feel, and how it changed her mind and body several years ago after it has made her stronger than she can ever imagine. After having gone through her very first transformations in 2008 and 2 more after 2 pregnancies in the last few years, she wants the world to know that there is hope for everyone to get in great shape whether or not they were dealt with not-so-good genes like she was.

What my work means to me

As somebody who has struggled with weight gain several years ago, I've been through a complex series of trial and error with my fitness and nutrition. So, just like any regular man and woman out there, I too have encountered difficulties in the fat loss department. The good news is: I don't hold back. I share all of my fat loss strategies with you because I want you to succeed – just like I did. Helping others who have trouble with fat loss is my passion. My biggest reward as a fitness coach is helping my clients get amazing results so they can live amazing lives. This is the driving force that motivates me to deliver the best health and fitness information to my clients every day and what gets me out of bed in the morning besides serving God and my family.

What my work means to others

I am in continued pursuit of cutting edge fitness and nutrition knowledge and research to keep things fun, exciting, and effective. This means that I am continually learning to enhance my knowledge about this industry so that we can give our clients the best results possible. This means that our clients can trust that they are getting the finest fitness advice that will fit their situation and their lifestyle.

Fuel Your Soul

by Mike Duffy

A woman's self-image has always been the most crucial thought they hold close to them. The media is always focusing on the ideal body for women. They put it in their heads that if you do not look like a runway model, movie star or Sports Illustrated cover girl, your self-worth goes down.

Many women fall victim to this ideal. The media plays a big part in marketing a certain body type, and they are constantly altering their version of what the ideal female body type should be. To be honest, the appropriate body image is just being healthy physically, mentally and comfortable in your own skin no matter what you weigh. However, the majority of women are discouraged by the dedication involved, get bad advice or give up because they want quicker results. A certain number will realize that their health is important, and if they get healthy first, then the weight will come off. It is then that they will be able to enjoy the life-long benefits.

Leanna Sheldon is one of the successful ones. She has been through it all since she was a teenager. She had her ups and downs as she went through self-doubt, discouragement, success, and failure. You name it, she has been through it. However, being the strong woman that Leanna is, she was finally able to stay fully focused on the mission to become healthy and lose weight. Because of her focus and hard work, she was able to lose an incredible 104 pounds and keep it off for the past 6 years! This is an accomplishment that may have sounded far-fetched in her earlier years of yo-yo dieting. After many tries, she felt that her goal was unattainable. When she finally came to the realization that she needed a better way than starvation diets and overtraining, that it would take months of dedication, not weeks, her mind shifted and she realized it was possible. Knowing it was possible was all she needed.

Her story started at about 15 years old. At that time, Leanna went through an extremely difficult breakup. Her issues with body image began with that breakup. She started becoming aware of her looks and weight. She became self-conscious and started to starve herself because she thought being thinner would make her more attractive to her ex-boyfriend. She was not eating much at all. After starving herself for some time, she started getting negative comments about her appearance. These comments hit home, and she was able to use this to motivate herself to start eating normally again.

Things were going fine until she turned 21 and started working at a country club serving food. She found herself indulging in all the great country club treats. Combine this with a non-existent workout routine and things started spiraling out of control. It was not until she decided to visit her new boyfriend at school (he is now her husband), that she realized her weight was out of control. She felt the need to compete with the younger college girls trying to steal her boyfriend. It was at this point that she decided to join Weight Watchers for the first time. Leanna lost about 10-15 lbs, and she felt a lot better about herself.

Eventually she started getting a little too comfortable and when we get comfortable, we lose track of our progress and stray away from our goals. We eventually start thinking, "Hey I'm doing pretty good, maybe a cheat day wouldn't hurt." Well that cheat day turn into another and those cheat days lead to cheat weeks and so on. This is exactly what happened to Leanna. She began to let herself go. She would binge eat on all the worst foods. Instead of going out with her friends, she would stay home and eat any type of food she could get her hands on-pizza, Chinese, Mexican, Italian, etc. It got to a point where she did not even realize the amount of weight she was gaining. When she would look at herself in the mirror, she would just think that this is who she was and that is that. Food became her comfort zone, and she was addicted to her comfort zone.

There were many things that she had to through when she was overweight that were completely embarrassing. Leanna wanted to go to the beach but she was embarrassed. She could barely squeeze behind and around the chair at her job as a dental assistant when she was working on a patient. This was not an issue just a short time ago. The more problems she had, the more she turned to food to help relax her.

The turning point for Leanna happened in 2010. Unfortunately, she was involved in a very bad car accident. During the accident, her pants split. It was completely embarrassing. She felt like she wanted to die. In Leanna's own words, "I knew I couldn't live like this anymore."

She got engaged shortly after the accident, and she set a goal to lose weight before the wedding. This completely motivated her, but she still had her struggles. On a routine doctor's visit, Leanna learned that she had high blood pressure. She thought that was a disease for older people, and she realized that if she did not change her lifestyle, her health status would continue to decline.

Leanna joined Weight Watchers for a second time because she felt their meetings were very helpful. She also joined a local personal training studio and took part in a 6-week body fat challenge. This program was different because they showed Leanna how to eat to be healthy and why she needed to eat this way. Learning what she needed to do to be successful for the rest of her life was enough to motivate her. She was tremendously determined, and six weeks later she had lost over 12% body fat and 20 pounds. Her determination to finally end the yo-yo dieting and take control of her health really got the ball rolling.

Leanna's confidence improved, and she felt unstoppable. For the first time, she was losing weight in a healthy manner - not starving but eating, not sitting home alone but attending boot camp classes and exercising. She worked hard at being consistent and in control, which, at times, affected personal relationships. Some of her friends could not accept the fact that she had to spend more time at the gym and not out with them. These are the type of sacrifices and changes she was dedicated to make.

There were still tough times, obstacles, and self-skepticism, but she had learned how to handle them. She continued to win over her demons and from 2011 to 2013 she lost a total of 104 pounds!

It has been over 6 years, and Leanna is still continuing to maintain her amazing weight loss. Leanna now competes in 5k and 10k races and has even run a few marathons! Talk about determination! This is something she never thought she could do. It is amazing what you can accomplish when you put your mind to it.

Leanna recently gave birth to her first child - a beautiful baby boy. She worked out throughout her entire pregnancy and had the support of her amazing husband. "My husband has supported me since day one. He loved me when I was overweight. He told me, I love you no matter what you look like because you never change inside."

The mixture of her work ethic, commitment, and loving support system helped fuel her soul and transform her body. Leanne advises everyone, "It is possible. You have to believe in yourself! You have to fight for yourself everyday but you are worth it!"

Before   *After*

ABOUT MIKE DUFFY

Mike Duffy is the owner of Mike Duffy's Personal Training Studios in New Jersey. Mike Graduated from Rutgers University in 1986 with a BS in Exercise Science and immediately opened up his first gym and began training clients. Mike was an accomplished bodybuilder for 12 years culminating his career by winning the Natural Mr. America in 1988 and placing 5th at the WABBA World Championships that same year.

After finishing up his bodybuilding career in 1988 he began power lifting. He won the New Jersey State Championship in 1991 and then took off from competing for the next 23 years to work on developing his personal training studios and help raise two beautiful children. He jumped back into competitive power lifting after a 23-year layoff in 2015 and won the WNPF National Championship and "Best Lifter" award while setting 2 National Records at the age of 53.

During his competitive hiatus, Mike opened 8 gyms and personal training studios where he worked as a personal trainer. He spent time getting his Post Rehab and Holistic Lifestyle Coaching Certifications. He also spent his time helping clients get healthy and into shape. Mike focuses on training weight loss clients, Post Rehab clients, training athletes and working as a holistic nutrition counselor.

Mike's biggest accomplishment was the development of his "6 Week Body Fat Challenge." For the last 19 years, he and his trainers have helped thousands of people lose up to 48.5 lbs and win up to $5,000 in only 6 short weeks. More importantly, this program has help people reduce their cholesterol, blood pressure, blood glucose, inflammation, improve digestive and autoimmune disorders and improve many other medical issues. Mike has given away over $120,000.00 in cash prizes during the last 10 years of the Challenge. "I like to focus on holistic nutrition and educating people how to eat properly, sensible training programs and the use of experienced coaching during the 6-week program. I also like to motivate my clients with prize money for placing in the top 3 of each 6-week event. The key to the success of this program and the results we produce for people is our nutrition plan. It consists of information learned from over 30 years of education, personal experience & research, trial and error and knowing that everyone is different and there is not one diet or training program that will work for everyone."

Transforming Your Body God's Way:

A Fitness Minister Shows You How

by Mike Echevarria

"Be careful what you think,
because your thoughts run your life."
(NCV) Pro 4:23

Great Thoughts, Great Results!

How you think and what you think will either make you or break you, regardless of whether you are a fitness trainer, teacher, police officer, lawyer, doctor, or an unemployed salesperson. It does not matter what your job is, your work will be affected by your thoughts. Regardless of who you are, your life will be affected by your thoughts.

Now I want to share a story from one of my boot campers, Sarah. Her thoughts were getting the best of her and she wasn't even realizing it. I'll let her explain it. She wrote me this after about a year at boot camp:

"A little over a year ago, I was shopping at Goodwill for clothes to get me by. I didn't feel like I was good enough to buy new clothes at the weight I was at. I told people I was "embracing my chubbiness" but the truth was that I was heartbroken. How had I let myself get to this point? The reflection in the mirror did not show who I wanted to be. Only a best friend would see through the smiles and chuckles. She asked me if I wanted to buy a few Group-ons to try out this boot camp over the summer. I hated exercise; I wrote the book on excuses! Somehow, I knew my friend wasn't really doing it for her, but a ploy to find my spark. I agreed to give it a try, for her of course.

> I had no idea that the first day would change my life forever! It was exciting, and hard, and challenging but I loved it! By the end of the first week, I had little muscles in my arms! That Groupon turned into a membership and a year-long commitment. A year later, my whole world has changed! Now I go to boot camp 3-6 times a week and would never dream of missing a session."

Her best friend who saw the charade that Sarah was putting on, decided to help her out by getting her to try out the boot camp. Now I know Sarah's personality. She is a very giving person and she was only doing this to appease her friend. Little did she know that her thoughts on exercise were going to change.

I don't openly tell people I am a Fitness Minister I just practice the Biblical principal of loving your neighbor and sharing truths of positivity and of course making the boot camp fun! So, when Sarah's thoughts of exercise changed and she actually saw results in the first week, she was on her way to transforming her life.

From personal experience, I know getting fit and staying fit is at least 90% mental. Our minds are instrumental in helping us achieve our goals. It is of the utmost importance to have the proper frame of mind if we are going to have the greatest chance to succeed. Let us read what the Word of God says in Romans chapter 12:*2a*:

> *Do not be conformed to this world (this age), [fashioned after and adapted to its external, superficial customs], but be transformed (changed) by the [entire] renewal of your mind [by its new ideals and its new attitude] (AMP)*
> *Rom 12:2a*

We see that renewal of the mind is changing the way we think with new ideals and a new attitude, which is God's perspective, not man's point of view. The Bible is letting us know the importance of having a good attitude and have the right ideals. Now, this applies in every area of life. Without the right perspective, how are we expected to accomplish our goals?

For example, I feel the first and most important step in achieving our goals, is to truly believe that we may, in fact, reach them. Now, I do not think we consciously set goals we believe we cannot reach, yet if we have the wrong perspective about our ability to attain these goals, many of us will have self-doubt about reaching our goals. This "wrong" thinking causes most people to quit their pursuit of getting fit.

Now let's get back to Sarah's story. I wanted to share her story because it shows how her original thoughts of exercise changed as she was immersed in a culture of positivity, encouragement and love.

> "It's Michael's outstanding leadership, motivation, and desire for everyone to be successful. He makes you feel like you're wanted there, valued, and important

to the boot camp. Michael explains every exercise, demonstrates the correct form, shows you the specific muscles you are targeting, and guides you as you go along. **My workouts with Michael are tough…but it's also fun. He has a way of pushing me to limits that I wouldn't be able to reach training on my own.**

This leads me to the Fitness by Example community. I have made new friends that encourage each other, support one another, and we all have a common goal. We look forward to seeing each other and hold each other accountable.

But it's also done so much for my health; my physician is amazed and impressed! Let's talk numbers. I started charting my results right away. The numbers don't lie:

Lost 35.8% Fat Mass (73.2 – 37.4)
Lost 15.6% Fat Percent (39.1 – 23.5)
Lost 5.3% BMI (31.2 – 25.9)
Lost 29 Pounds (190 – 161)
Lost 3 jean sizes (16, now 10)
Gained 7.79lbs of Fat Free Muscle (114.21, now 122)

I've lost weight, lowered my body fat and gained muscle, but most importantly, I feel better about myself. As all this was accomplished, so was a physical and emotional transformation. Now as I begin my second year, I am happier, stronger, healthier, with noticeable increased energy levels. I have achieved my personal goals and much more. **This is truly a**

life changing experience and if you're ready for the commitment, join the journey, come aboard!"

Now I know I did not go over specific training routines, though I can tell you that my boot camp is 90% body weight exercises. You can find training programs and nutrition plans everywhere! This was not the point. The focus is on changing your thought pattern. Sarah is a perfect example of many of us who are afraid of changing. Yet, she changed her thought process, took a leap of faith and realized her dreams—she didn't hit rock bottom, she soared like an eagle. You want permanent, life altering transformation? It begins with your thoughts. Take action by changing your thoughts today!

About Mike Echevarria

Michael Echevarria is the owner and founder of Fitness By Example in Winter Park, Florida. Michael is a 35+ year fitness veteran. He began lifting back in 1978 and first competed in powerlifting in 1981. Michael was a three -time Air Force powerlifting champion, 1984-86. He began training for bodybuilding in 1996, which is when he started to study and apply the principles of body transformation and fat loss, especially stubborn body fat. In 2001 Michael earned his certification as a fitness trainer. His passion in life is to empower people with the truth, in the area of physical fitness.

Michael is an accomplished and serious business owner who gives back to his community. Fitness By Example partners with the Christian Sharing Center every year to provide a Thanksgiving Turkey Day workout. Over the past 4 Thanksgiving FBE boot camp has donated turkeys and gift cards to feed over 360 families. He also serves as a fitness minister, where he teaches a boot camp at Northland Church with a devotional afterwards. Michael is married with two children and one grandchild.

I Didn't Think I Could Get Back Up, But I Did....

by Shawn Eichorn

As I looked through the bars in the jail cell I shook my head in disbelief. I was only twenty-three years old and I had just gotten my second DWI.

I got up and looked in the mirror. I was hungover. I felt horrible and I looked even worse.

My stomach was hanging over my belt and my body was miserably out of shape. All from five plus years of partying and overeating after high school.

I knew I had to make a change in my life or I wouldn't live to see age thirty.

In high school I was center on the hockey team and captain on the football team. Lifting weights and exercising was important to me to stay in shape to compete in the sports I loved.

So, going back to the gym was no big deal for me. After signing up at the local YMCA I decided to stop by GNC to look around for some supplements and some new motivation.

I picked up a magazine called Muscle Media to inspire me. Inside was tons of information on how to get back in shape. But the one thing that caught my eye was a 12-Week nationwide transformation contest called "Body for Life".

There was also a book with the same title. I picked it up and devoured it. I don't believe I had read a book since high school but I finished it in one day.

Inside were true stories of ordinary people who had achieved amazing transformations through exercise and proper nutrition. Their before and after pictures inspired me. I knew that if these people could achieve tremendous results that I certainly could – especially with the athleticism and genetics I had been given.

I decided to enter the contest. Here's how it changed my life.

First, I made the conscious decision that I was going to change. I was not happy with my life and I knew that I was better than what I was doing with it. I made a promise to myself that I would finish the 12-week program no matter what obstacles I ran into.

Second, I put some positive pressure on myself. In order to successfully qualify for the grand prize in the contest you had to submit a before and after picture with your 12-week results. I immediately took FIVE before pictures for motivation.

I put one on my refrigerator, one by the speedometer in my car, on my dresser, the mirror in the bathroom and on one my office desk. Everywhere I looked there was a reminder of the unsuccessful life that I had created for myself.

To further enhance the positive pressure, I called a photographer and scheduled a photo session with her. I set it exactly after my 12-week program was to be finished.

I knew how important goal setting was from competing in sports in high school. Before I set my goals I had to get some before measurements to find out where I was starting from. So, I scheduled a complementary session with one of the trainers at the YMCA to take some measurements.

After my session with her I sat down and wrote out my 12-week goals.

1. To quit drinking by the end of the 12-week program.

2. Lose five inches off of my waist

3. To finish the program

4. To be able to see my abs

5. Get my body fat below 7%.

6. To finish as one of the finalist in the contest

Next, I designed my program. In order to finish the 12 weeks I had to keep the program simple. I lifted weights on Mondays, Wednesday & Fridays to help increase my muscle mass (metabolism boosting). On Tuesday, Thursday & Saturday mornings I performed aerobic workouts to help optimize fat loss.

I always took one day off as a rest day and a cheat day with my nutrition program.

I also made the decision that I would get up at five am before work each day to accomplish my workouts.

The first few weeks of the program were the most challenging. Trying to establish new habits and getting rid of the old ones was difficult. But I overcame the challenges with the belief that when finished the program my life would change around. And soon those challenges established discipline in my life which then created structure. And structure gave me the path to succeed.

During the sixth week of the program is when I decided to quit drinking for the rest of the program. At the end of the week I didn't consume one drop of alcohol. It was the first time in eight years that I had gone through a weekend without drinking.

Coincidently that's when I really starting noticing a tremendous, positive change in my body.

The fat around my midsection was peeling off week after week. Almost effortlessly.

I started wearing tight tank tops and short shorts to the gym because the definition in my body was amazing. I loved how my muscles looked. Even as I was getting smaller I actually looked bigger in the mirrors at the gym because my body fat was getting so low.

I was getting compliments every day from complete strangers on how good I looked. My confidence shot through the roof and my whole attitude on life completely changed.

At the end of the twelve week contest I had totally changed my body and life. I went from being overweight and having uncertainty in my life to a healthy, fit person with total confidence. I knew that I could achieve anything in life with my new body.

I achieved all of my goals that I had set for myself.

1. I quit drinking

2. I lost 5 ½ inches off my waist

3. I finished the 12-week program

4. My body fat dropped to 6.8%

5. I was able to see my abs

6. I finished as one of the top 2,000 finalists in the contest that year

Finishing the 12-week program, along with the way my body looked, gave me the **CONFIDENCE** and the **BELIEF** that I could accomplish anything in my life.

I decided that I wanted to help other people feel the way I felt after the contest. I felt that every human on earth should get the opportunity to feel confident, strong and healthy.

I also knew that I had found my calling in life. The only subject that ever interested me in high school was physical education and sports. Becoming a personal trainer seemed like a natural fit for me.

I immediately sent out a press release to the local paper about my accomplishment. They interviewed me and put a big article in the paper with my before and after picture.

From the article, I got my first six clients. I was making more money training them each week than I was at my full time (ordinary) job. So, I quit and started my training career.

My transformation has given me so much in life.

Before my transformation, I was a person who worked a dead-end job and was partying on weekends to drown my unsatisfying life. Now I have a career. A career that makes my life happy.

First, I love what I do. I have a passion to help people. I get up every morning and help people improve their bodies which helps improve their life. It doesn't get any better than that.

Second, it creates more time for me. With more time, I can work less and do the things I enjoy like playing sports and spending time with my wife and two children.

Third, I make more money. Having more money gives me the opportunity to give more to my family. I can take them on vacations or buy them new toys if they want. This makes me feel joyful to be able to do that.

And it creates security for us. I have money in my savings account so that if something should happen we are prepared for it. It also is the security to know that we will have money when my wife and I retire and have money for my children when they go off to college.

All of this success is because I made the decision to change and I made myself my number one priority in my life. If you're reading my transformation success story right now and you're thinking about making a transformation for yourself – do it. You are worth it!

About Shawn Eichorn

Shawn Eichorn has been a professional fitness trainer and owner of Fitness Success Personal Training since 2000. In the past 17 years, he has helped over 2,300 people become the best versions of themselves. He believes that anyone can improve their life through with education on fitness and nutrition.

If you would like to contact Shawn you can give him a call at Fitness Success at 507-206-4126 or visit his website at Rochester-PersonalTrainer.com

Becoming a SuperFit Family

by Val Fujii and Alicia Blumert

Val Fujii and Alicia Blumert

Our journey to being a SuperFit Family started back in January 2014 when we found a SuperKidz Homeschool Fitness class. The kids were getting an amazing workout twice per week and each time I dropped them off, I noticed signs in the window for a Ladies Bootcamp. I peeked through the window a few times while they were working out and also saw the wall of fame of all the campers who had experienced results from this program. I was intimidated to say the least and afraid to take the plunge. Maybe the words "boot camp" held me back! "Not for me," I thought.

So, for 2 YEARS I watched through that window. I attended a local gym, tried to stay on track, even hired a personal trainer a few times, but ever since we moved, I had not found my new niche. I had left a solid routine back home, and I missed my trainer and the gym I used to attend. I was starting to get frustrated and was not happy with where I was.

In June of 2012, I made a huge turning point in my health and wellness. After my husband's brain tumor surgery in January, I made a commitment to myself and my family that I would no longer live in chronic pain and decided to get in the best shape of my life so that I could better take care of my family. The stress of the surgery and the recovery got the best of my post-surgery lower back, and my sciatica started to flare up again. Paul got back to work, looked and felt great, and now it was my turn to pay attention to my health. I had finished PT, joined a gym, hired a trainer, started eating healthy and taking proper supplementation, and truly got in the best shape of my life! I even started helping friends and family get healthy, too. After we moved, though, I started to lose that momentum. I was homesick, missed my family and friends, and was truly overwhelmed.

My frustration drove me to face my fears, and in December of 2015, I finally decided to try a free introductory class at SuperFit. That decision was one of the hardest ones I ever made! Things like BOOTCAMPS, 5Ks, and SPORTS just weren't part of my childhood, for sure, and I really felt like it wasn't "me" at all. I was always afraid to step out. I played basketball and soccer in Jr High/High school but really only played because the competition wasn't high! However, now was the time to punch fear in the face! What motivated me? A WAKE UP CALL that last July.

We got the call that my husband's brain cancer had returned. Three days later, Paul was in surgery having a brain tumor removed that was now a stage 3. In an instant, our world turned upside down and the stress went through the roof. At that moment, yes, I was MUCH stronger than I ever had been and definitely felt the difference between how my body and emotions handled the stress between then and the original diagnosis in Nov 2011. However, I knew that it was, once again, time to step it up because this time, we were about to embark on the unknown - A YEAR LONG ROAD of CHEMO AND RADIATION. We acted

QUICKLY, as advised by our friend, Kate Burke. She had a 10-year victory with a Glioblastoma multiforme (aggressive malignant brain tumor). She lived for 10 years with a tumor that normally calls for a 1-2 year life span. I am forever grateful for her because even though she was not "here," I heard her words echo through my heart. "Don't wait. Act Quickly. Get Treatment." We did. That year was one of the most challenging, heart wrenching, lonely, sad, depressing times in our lives but we held on to our faith in God and believed for the best! (Isaiah 40:31)

Joining SuperFit Camps that December was my way of punching cancer in the face and saying, "You are NOT going to get the best of me! I WILL fight and be strong for my husband. I WILL have joy in the midst of pain and be that strength for our kids!"

I worked hard and stayed consistent through the challenging workouts that Val Fujii, and his team, offered at his camps. I learned so much about nutrition through his amazing program within the gym called "The 28 Day Transformation Challenge." I focused in on a goal and decreased my body fat and weight. I actually became the SuperFit Challenge Champion that Spring! I won gift cards, a Champion jacket, and an amazing incentive trip for my family to a beautiful resort in Lake Tahoe! We were able to go for my birthday weekend, and we enjoyed every minute, making memories with our family. Life was kept pretty simple because of my husband's energy levels during chemotherapy, so winning this trip meant everything to us and was the best birthday "gift" ever!

The best part of winning that challenge was that I began to feel comfortable in my own skin again and felt a renewed HOPE. I looked forward to going to camp each day and being surrounded by happy, encouraging people. I would arrive at camp with tears in my eyes, but leave class with a smile on my face! Those are PRICELESS RESULTS that you cannot purchase through a "packaged program." It only comes from the culture you choose to be a part of. SuperFit is like family to us now.

Today, my husband has gained his strength back after completing treatment! He is now a SuperFit camper! As a matter of fact, we are a SuperFit family since our kids still attend SuperKidz. Paul is excited as he is building stamina and muscle tone back. He started off barely able to make it through a workout to now going 3 times per week! Val is so good about working with him to modify as needed. We are forever grateful to Val and the SuperFit Team for the difference they've made in our lives. Thank you, SUPERFIT!!!

Before   *After*

ABOUT VAL FUJII

I've always been active and have played various sports since I was a young child. My true passion is tennis, which I began playing when I was only 5 years old. My father, who was a sports fanatic himself, would always come watch me play and support me. He was never physically active, but after his first bypass in 1985, he had to make changes to his nutrition and start exercising. He decided to follow the doctor's orders and started an exercise program which was simply walking around the block of our neighborhood, increasing his distance a little at a time, and working his way up to walking 4 miles a day. He chose to do this to be here for his family. He made a decision to work out every day and change his diet. His diet consisted eating more vegetables, fruits and lean protein such as fish and chicken. He lost weight and maintained this lifestyle for some years. He was religious with this new lifestyle which gave him another 10 years before his next bypass surgery. After his second surgery in 1995, he continued this healthy lifestyle. Walking, which was his only form of exercise became difficult, and painful in 2007. He started to worry if he would be able to continue walking, which he enjoyed so much. So, I designed a strength training, flexibility and joint mobility program which helped him immensely. With his new exercise program, he continued walking again.

This was truly inspiring to me that he did the best he could to live life to the fullest. My mother told me on January 3rd, 2012 for the first time my father didn't complete his workout program, which was very unusual of him. He told my mom that he was too tired to finish. He passed away the very next day at the age of 83 after living a very active life for his age. His life inspires me to help others with their fitness so they can live life to the fullest like my Dad did.

Certified National Academy of Sports Medicine Personal Trainer (NASM PT) and a Performance Enhance Specialist (PES). As a certified Tennis Professional with the United States Professional Tennis Association (USPTA), he was able to compete as the head coach, fitness trainer and tennis player for the American Samoa Tennis Team in the 2015 Pacific Games in Papua, New Guinea, a multi-sport event, much like the Olympic Games, with participation exclusively from countries around the South Pacific Ocean.

Currently the owner of SuperFit Camps.

THE EMOTIONAL WHY

by Julian Gaylor

Just making goals is useless…

Hear me out.

In my 11 years of helping people improve their life through health and wellness, I have concluded that just setting a goal has very little impact on someone succeeding. The real factor that defines success is if the individual has, what I call, an *emotional why*.

An *Emotional WHY* is the deep down, burning desire WHY you want to change. It is the thing that once you find it, makes you get out of bed at 4am to work out without even thinking about hitting snooze. It is the thing that makes you look at that piece of chocolate cake at the party and think "Not a chance in the world." It is the thing that makes you feel like you could walk through a brick wall if it was standing in the way of you and your *emotional why*. Once you find your *emotional why,* you are near unstoppable.

An *emotional why* isn't to lose 10kg, fit back into those favorite jeans or even to look amazing on your wedding day. Your *emotional why* is a step beyond that and has some real and raw emotion attached to it. For example:

*I want to lose 10kg (**goal**) because I want to feel confident and happy at social functions. Right now, I don't feel like I fully throw myself into social events as I am embarrassed with my body. Instead I want to be able to have fun and be proud. (**emotional why**)

*I want to fit back into my favorite pair of jeans (**goal**) because those jeans remind me of the free spirit I used to be. I want to relive those days and the adventure and fun that came with it. (**emotional why**)

*I want to look amazing on my wedding day (**goal**) because ever since I was a little girl, I've dreamed of being that beautiful bride in her perfect dress walking down the aisle towards the man of my dreams. I nearly cry every time I see it in the movies, and I want my day to be just like that. (**emotional why**)

Now you can see the difference between a goal and an emotional why. Let me share a story about one of my clients who had one of the most powerful emotional why's I have ever experienced.

Her name is Sue. Sue was 59 years old, very overweight had type 2 diabetes and blood pressure through the roof. She basically just came to me straight from her doctor. She said to me "My doctor says I have to lose weight." When I asked her why she wanted to lose the weight, with her arms crossed, she proclaimed. "Oh, he (Doctor) says I've got to do it, so I'd better do it."

I had to ask her a few more questions to dig a little deeper because I honestly could not help Sue if she was simply here because her doctor said so. After asking a few more questions of her, I finally asked, "Okay Sue, if you lost 10kg-15kg you'd certainly have a lot more energy. How would life be better if you had more energy?" I saw her pause for a moment, and her body language changed. Her eyes welled up a little. This is the moment where magic happened for Sue.

She said, "My daughter Sarah, has a three-month old called Max. She's a single mum and she's got to work. I'm scared that I'm not going to be

72

able to help her. I'm scared that I'm going to die or I'm going to be sick, and then Sarah has got to look after me while trying to work and look after Max."

At that point, she was in tears and THAT was her *emotional why*. She wanted to see her grandson grow up. She wanted to see her daughter be able to provide for Max and live her own life. Sue did NOT want to burden Sarah by becoming so sick that she was dependent on her. You can see how that is so much more powerful than, "I need to lose 10kg."

I can tell you now that every time Sue had to dig deep in a workout or she was on the brink of binge eating, she went back to her *emotional why*. She remembered this was for Sarah and little Max. She wanted to give them every chance at a happy life and that included a happy, healthy Mother/Grandmother.

Fast forward around 6 months and Sue had lost 19kg. Her diabetes and blood pressure issues were history. She was healthy, happy and a hero in my eyes. Sue had been looking after Max a lot while Sarah was working, and one of the most rewarding moments of my training career was when Sue called me out of the blue. She was crying. "Jules, I needed to call you right away"

I'm thinking, "What's going on? What's wrong? Something's happened."

Through the crying, there was a little laugh. "Max just said Gamma(Grandma)"

In that moment, she realized it might never have happened if she had not made a change. Small moments like this are what I consider the epitome of an emotional why.

Just remember, no one else can decide your *emotional* why. I don't care if someone thinks it is silly, superficial or insignificant, it is yours and yours alone. So take some time to sit down and look inward.

What is it that you truly want? What is your *emotional why?*

ABOUT JULIAN GAYLOR

Julian Gaylor is a Health and Wellness coach that believes *real world* behaviors and skills have more to do with successful weight loss and body transformation than any training program or diet ever will. Julian's 11 years in the industry started in his hometown of Ballarat, a small city in Victoria, Australia. Julian helped his local residents lose over 1000kg(2200lb) and most importantly, taught his clients how to keep it off and live happy and healthy forever.

After selling his private studio, Julian moved on to working with personal trainers and fitness businesses owners around the world. Thriving off seeing others succeed, he showed them how to grow their own businesses and ultimately how to change the lives of their clients in a positive way.

Julian is now managing one of the biggest gyms in Melbourne, Australia and reaching out to the masses with regular public speaking, a radio segment called *Real World Health and Wellness* and providing free content on social media platforms. Over his career, he has changed the course of many lives for the better and continues to do so with his down to earth and simple strategies that anyone can adapt into their life.

I AM A SURVIVOR

by Joe Green

*"Today's adversity prepares us
for the challenges of tomorrow."*
-Joe Green

I am a son, a brother and a friend. I am a father, a teacher and a motivator. I am what I teach, because I am a survivor.

Several years ago, I almost lost my life in a near fatal car accident. I left work early and was on my way home. I was stopped at an intersection waiting to make a left turn. I looked in the rearview mirror and saw a school bus approaching. I continued to watch oncoming traffic and took one last glance in the rearview mirror. That happened to be just moments before I was hit.

My car was destroyed and my health, as I once knew it, was forever changed. The school bus rear ended my car, rode up over the trunk and then up over the passenger's side roof smashing the majority of the car into the ground. By the time I had emerged from the twisted sheet metal and broken glass, I realized that I was badly injured. I suffered injuries to my neck, back, hips and legs.

I had to start all over again -walking, sitting, standing and becoming active. I knew that I was facing the greatest challenge of my life. Constant pain and physical therapy sessions that ended in pure exhaustion was the norm for months and months. I would end up missing many months of work. Unable to drive or do much else. It hurt just to exist.

Outside of therapy I was tired and inactive. The extra pounds seemingly piled on by the minute. There I was, overweight and wondering how I was ever going to recover.

The attending physician that I had also happened to be a friend who I used to see in the gym working out. I remember sitting in his office, scared and in pain. The most memorable day of my life was the day he told me that I had a choice. He said I could go through physical therapy and recover to about 60% of full range of motion and physical activity, or I could choose to fight and demand more of myself in hopes of recovering to about 80% of full recovery.

This clearly required a commitment on a whole different level. Knowing that I was facing the biggest obstacle of my life, I chose the greatest challenge I could think of. I decided to try bodybuilding, figuring that would get me back to 100% recovery and in the best shape of my life. That was a truly pivotal decision.

It was not easy. It was painful, and I wanted to quit just about every day. In the beginning, it was frustrating, to say the least. There was no such thing as the Internet, and I had no access to personal trainers. I recall asking a few guys I knew, who were into bodybuilding, for help. They dismissed me with poor advice so I had to find my own way.

Determined, I turned to magazines and articles and researched as much as I could. Meanwhile I continued on with physical therapy. As time passed, it seemed as though the more I learned, the better I felt. I got back into the gym. I worked out when I knew the gym would be almost vacant so that I could focus and workout without interruption. Soon, I pushed past old limitations, got a firm grip on the pain and found myself in legitimate pursuit of a new and improved version of myself that I never dreamed possible.

My goal, my results, my journey - it was personal. I lost over 50 pounds and went from barely walking to sprinting through vigorous cardiovascular workouts and carving out a hand- crafted physique, forged out of pure grit and determination. I reshaped my entire body from head to toe and transformed my whole entire lifestyle. I went from competing for the ability to stand upright for five minutes to competing in an all-natural bodybuilding contest where I took second place.

I missed first place by just a couple of points, but I exceeded all of my goals. I made the biggest comeback of my life.

Sure, I'm really proud of the trophies from the competition but what I am most proud of is the transformation from ruin to peak health.

I know firsthand what it's like to battle back, to fight for what you want. I understand how hard it is to continue on when uncertainty is the only thing you see when you look to the future. Because I know the taste of despair and challenge, I have enjoyed the taste of success. But it's not over for me, because I still suffer from chronic pain every single day thanks to that accident many years ago.

Despite that, I am still a son, a brother and a friend. I am still a father, a teacher and a motivator. I am an example of total body transformation from head to toe, inside and out. I am what I teach, I am inspiration and I am transformation because I am a survivor.

ABOUT JOE GREEN

Joe started his personal training business in 1996 providing specialty exercise programs for women, mature to senior adults and sports specific training for competitive athletes. Later in January of 2000 he launched his personal training business into the medical community. Since that time, Joe has become recognized in his local community as the expert people trust and the one doctors refer to for his work with post rehab and movement disorder populations.

His philosophies, training methodology and skill set are at the leading edge of performance training with a focus on a simple foundation and premise for exercise variety intended to affect steady and consistent progress over time.

Joe's evolving programs, educational seminars and growing network of medical professionals has created a collaborative and mutually supportive bond which continues to yield some of the best long term results available today.

IT TAKES FAITH

by Randy Hartz

It was November 20, 2001. I was 28 years old and, on the outside, it looked like I had reached success and had it all together. I was a business owner, a national champion bodybuilder and had achieved most of the dreams I had set for myself.

That day, I walked out of the post office and was told to get on the ground as I was under arrest. Everything was happening in slow motion. I remember sitting in the police car feeling this strange sense of peace. I always wondered how things would end. Either dead or arrested. The lie was finally over.

The good news was that I could remove the mask and figure out who I was and why I was put here on Earth. The bad news was that I was arrested for drug trafficking and was facing some serious charges.

The question I had to answer was, "How did I end up here?" I was raised with morals and knew the difference between right and wrong. As I reflected on my life I remember growing up looking in the muscle magazines and thinking that these guys had it all. Fame, power, girls, money, and everything else that came along with it. I formed an image of what success looked like to me, and I started down the path of creating it. As I went through college I started using steroids to help me accomplish my dream of becoming a professional bodybuilder. It was only going to be for six weeks, then I was going to quit.

During that six weeks, my body changed dramatically but something else happened. I started getting more attention. This started to affect me, and I became obsessed with what others thought about me. There wasn't a physical addiction but psychologically I was hooked. That was the beginning of a life long journey of battling with self-image issues.

I ended up spending 3 ½ years in prison which, looking back, was the best thing that ever could have happened to me. It gave me time to get my priorities in line. Before, it was money and me…or was it me then money? They both fought for the pole position. Now it's Faith, Family, Fitness, and Finances.

The day I went to prison, my son, Noah, was 6 weeks old. The attorney said he was going to get me out on probation, but 8 weeks in he quit returning our phone calls. I was in Florida, 2000 miles away from home, so I didn't see my wife and son again until he was 8 months old. I remember going back to my cell and thinking about committing suicide. I felt like my wife needed to move on so they could have a normal life. I prayed and told God what my plan was. He either showed me what to do next or the only solution I had was the easy way out.

A few days later I was walking down the hallway and found a magazine that just *happened* to be leaning up against the wall. It was about faith and I picked it up and started paging through it. I got to the end and something told me to write them and ask for help. Here is what I said.

"I'm an inmate in Florida State Penitentiary. I have no money to give you but if you can send me a Bible study or something that will help me better understand how to trust God, I will pay it back some day."

They sent me a study called Bible Faith, and I devoured it. It was exactly what I was looking for and it totally changed my life.

Within a few months, God intervened in my situation and my sentence was dropped in half! I still had a couple of years left to serve, but there was light at the end of the tunnel. I ended up transferring back to my home state of South Dakota to serve the remainder of my time so my wife and son could come and visit more often.

During this time, I poured myself into personal development by reading the Bible, books on personal development and any other spiritual books I could get my hands on. I was like a sponge.

I got out of prison in November of 2005. Melissa and I were completely starting over in life and living in my in-laws' basement. I drove an old beat up car that my mother-in-law gave me. Thankfully, it was gray so the duct tape holding on the bumper matched the paint.

It was tough at first because nobody wanted to give me an opportunity. I remember going into a job placement center and filling out an application and the young guy behind the counter smugly said that they can't help people with felonies. I can accept policies, but there is a right and wrong way to treat people.

Instead of getting discouraged, I used it to motivate me.

God began to open doors, and I got a job working for a guy at my Church who owned a construction company. He taught me a lot more about life than anything. My heart was to get back into fitness but my wife was nervous that I would fall back into my old lifestyle. I had to prove myself and regain her trust, which I understood.

One day she was working out at a friend's gym, and he mentioned that he could use some help. Melissa called me right away and said, "I think you are ready to get back into fitness."

That weekend I went to his gym and cleaned the whole place. I scrubbed the locker rooms and everything else without him asking or even knowing. He happened to walk in as I was finishing up, and I earned a job.

I remember the first week training one woman for free, and I was asking God how I was going to feed my family. That Friday, I ended up introducing another trainer to the Lord, and I knew I was right where I needed to be.

Today I own the gym that I used to train out of and have built a nutrition business that has helped us create a life that I never dreamed possible. We not only have financial freedom, but the time to do what we were put on Earth for.

I am so grateful that I was set aside for reason to understand that it's not about success, fame, fortune or what others think about me. I am priceless to God and once I got that, everything else took care of itself.

ABOUT RANDY HARTZ

Randy Hartz, owner of Complete Fitness, has been a Fitness Professional for 21 years helping 100s of Sioux Falls area residents look better, feel better, and perform better.

He began his career after graduating from SDSU with a degree in Exercise Science. He became an expert in fitness, nutrition, and overall health with a passion to help others improve their quality of life.

Randy specializes in fat loss for busy women in their 30s to 50s. He learned how fitness and nutrition work through his own journey of being a national champion bodybuilder.

He is passionate about fitness but it comes second next to his wife Melissa and 3 sons; Noah, Nick, and Max.

It's Never Too Late

by Kevin and Dr. Kristen Harvey

Anne Marie Spencer proved it is never too late to start caring for your body, health, and life. Her story is a 20-year long journey filled with battles of emotion and dedication to fitness.

Her entire life, Anne Marie had always struggled with her weight. Binge eating was her emotional crutch. Any time a crisis in her life arose, she would revert to binge-eating, making her feel worse, which led to another binge. And the cycle continued.

"The first major episode was in grade school when I skipped a couple grades and became an instant outcast among all students," Anne Marie said. "After this, I was fat until graduation."

Anne Marie's weight fluctuated when she went to college and "got her act together." She bounced around between 155 to 165 pounds, but lacked muscle tone and athletic ability. Then her 20's hit. Divorce. Job Loss. Her life was falling apart before her eyes, and her weight ballooned to 215 pounds.

"With no full-length mirrors in my house, and the ability to wear stretchy clothes to work, I had no idea how out of shape I'd become until I saw a photo of myself with some co-workers," Anne Marie said. "I seriously thought, 'who is that fat girl?' When I realized, it was me, I didn't even want to leave the house. I was disgusted."

That was her wake up call.

"I realized that not only was I hurting myself and my health, but I may literally be shortening my life, and for what? Food?" Anne Marie said. "It struck me how ridiculous it all was. I felt ugly. I couldn't wear the clothes I wanted to. My confidence was at an all-time low, and I realized that none of this was who I was."

"I wasn't fat. I just had extra fat. And I had to let the 'me' that I truly was out of this bulgy, slow, sedentary body."

Her first 20 pounds were lost quickly, and she said she admits it was done unhealthily, but it got her started on her fitness journey. Nutrition was her first step. She started watching what she ate with no exercise component added. She got down to 170 pounds. Although she said she felt better, she didn't feel like she was anywhere near her true potential.

She found an exercise class she enjoyed and started going four to five times a week. She started running, getting up earlier, and working out at home. "I found that getting up an hour earlier carved out a window of time that no one could take from me," Anne Marie said. "Sure, I could sleep in, but if I didn't get my exercise in each morning, I had no one to blame but myself."

Anne Marie stayed on track and worked her way up to finishing a half marathon. But, she hated it. At that point, she was around 153 pounds, 23 percent body fat, and had decent muscle tone, yet she still felt unfulfilled. She still had not reached her full potential.

Her life changed when she found Spartan Racing. She did not really know anything about it until she saw a competition on TV in 2015. The next day, she filled a bucket full of rocks and hiked to the top of the hill behind her home. "It was exhilarating to get to the top," Anne Marie said. "Best of all, there was running, but it was interrupted by all these cool tests of strength and endurance along the way. I realized that this was a test of fitness in every way it can be tested, and it would take a really well-rounded athlete to do well."

At that moment, she decided to sign up for her first race. She joined a Facebook group, Spartan 4-0, for Spartan racers over 30 years old. She also joined a local boot camp in Chattanooga, Scenic City Boot Camp & Transformation Center, and immediately fell in love with the training.

Her first race in Ft. Campbell, KY came and went. She finished the 4+ mile course in 2 hours and 15 minutes, coming in at the top 20 in her age group.

"I was ecstatic….and hooked," Anne Marie said. "I started training harder, and added an online obstacle course called Yancy Camp to my roster. I was doing that in the morning at 5 a.m., going to boot camp at 5 p.m., and running on the weekends."

Anne Marie completely retrained the way she ran from heel striking to forefoot striking making her faster. She studied nutrition habits of athletes, consulted with elite Spartan racers on how to "eat to perform," then she was ready to race.

In 2016, she completed a Spartan Trifecta-one Sprint (23-5 miles), a Super race (8-12 miles), a Beast race (14+ miles); and then one year later she "anniversaried" the Fort Campbell race by taking 45 minutes off her time, finishing first in her age group, and qualifying for the obstacle course racing world championships. Along the way, she became immersed in proper nutrition - not just what to eat to build muscle and shred fat, but when to eat it. She started to drop weight and body fat.

People noticed.

"The amazing thing was, I was doing okay, but it took Spartan to really focus my effort," Anne Marie said. "I suddenly wasn't obsessed on looking a certain way, but rather performing a certain way. I won't say it got easy, but it certainly helped."

"My fitness journey from that sad, sedentary, newly divorced girl to the athletic woman I am today took a total of 20 years. I look (and essentially am) younger now than then. I love fitness, and most of all helping others discover their fitness passion. The thing that hurts me the most is when people say they're 'too old to start.'"

For Anne Marie, she didn't reach her elite level of athleticism until she was well past 40 years old. She had high blood pressure. She had the beginnings of a heart issue. But today, none of that exists.

"Find your fitness passion," Anne Marie said. "It may take a while, but find a physical activity you really love. Try a variety of classes. Try running with friends. Just do something. You'll find it, and when you do, it ignites a passion to do better and better, and everything you need to do to get there will become your focus. Just start. Don't wait."

Each year, Anne Marie sets her bar higher. This year, she'll complete the Breckenridge Beast, which goes from 8-10,000 feet in elevation, compete in the Obstacle Course Racing World Championships.

"There's even talk of obstacle racing going to the Olympics," Anne Marie said. "And though I'm probably past the age curve of most Olympic athletes, don't count me out just yet."

No matter where you are in your life, you can start your transformation today. Like Anne Marie, it is never too late to start. Like Anne Marie, don't wait to find your fitness passion.

This chapter was written by Katelyn Clark.

ABOUT KATELYN CLARK

Katelyn Clark is the marketing manager for Scenic City Boot Camp and Transformation Center, owned by Kevin and Dr. Kristen Harvey. Scenic City Boot Camp is a group fitness training facility specializing in body transformation for men and women. Since coming to work for SCBC in 2016, Katelyn has transformed her body from 25% to 18% body fat and gained lean muscle while attending and following the SCBC programs. She has a B.S. in Corporate Communications and a double minor in professional writing and communication arts.

For the past 10 years, Scenic City Boot Camp has helped transform thousands of people's bodies and lives with their group training and nutrition coaching programs. But fitness wasn't always easy for Kevin or Kristen. Both pursued careers in fitness after transforming their own bodies. Kevin put on 35 lbs. of muscle during his freshman year in college, while Kristen lost over 40 lbs. her last year in physical therapy school. Their transformations completely changed the course of both their lives and as a result- have dedicated their entire lives to helping transform yours.

Scenic City Boot Camp is based in Chattanooga, Tn but they also offer online fitness coaching programs through their website, www.sceniccitybootcamp.com. They plan to launch a luxury fitness retreat offering in Mexico in the next year for those looking for a unique vacation experience. For more info, e-mail them at support@sceniccitybootcamp.com.

You can also visit their new online store, www.mysweatequitee.com, where you can purchase fitness t-shirts, tanks and hoodies designed to uplift and empower women. 10% of all profits go directly to non-profit organizations that help in the rescue efforts of Syrian refugees.

ABOUT KEVIN AND DR. KRISTEN HARVEY

Referred to as the "unstoppable husband and wife team" by Blush Magazine, Kevin and Dr. Kristen Harvey are the owners of Scenic City Boot Camp and Transformation Center in Hixson, TN. In the last 10 years, they-along with their team, have helped transform thousands of people's bodies and lives with their group training programs. But fitness wasn't always easy for Kevin or Kristen. Both pursued careers in fitness after transforming their own bodies. Kevin put on 35 lbs. of muscle during his freshman year of college, while Kristen lost over 40 lbs. during her last year in graduate school for physical therapy. Their transformations completely changed the course of both their lives and as a result- have dedicated their entire lives to helping transform yours.

While they are locally based, they offer online training programs that help clients look the way they want to look and feel the way they want to feel from the comfort of their home. To learn more about Scenic City Boot Camp's online programs, visit www.sceniccitybootcamp.com or e-mail support@sceniccitybootcamp.com. You can also find a link to their Sweat Equitee store, where they sell fitness t-shirts that empower women. 10% of all profits made from the t-shirts go to a charity that helps Yazidi women in Syria who are captured by ISIS to escape and rebuild their lives.

A MODERN DAY MENSCH

by Billy Hofacker

Andrew Sherman

As soon as I met Andy, I knew I liked him. He is the father of two teenage girls and has been married for 22 years. He is extremely charitable, donating his time and money to causes that are near and dear to him. Andy sits on the board at his temple and would certainly be considered a "mensch," the Yiddish word for person of character and integrity. He loves the things that matter, like family. While he can be serious when he needs to be, he does not take himself too seriously. While he is open and honest, he is also comical, often joking around and making the most of life's situations. Andy believes that laughter is the greatest medicine there is, and I happen to agree.

Before coming to us, Andy had everything one would need in physical terms. You wouldn't necessarily find him on the cover of Forbes, but he made a decent living. As CFO of a health publishing company for the past 17 years, he spends his days analyzing financial data.

While Andy had a nice house, beautiful family, and a solid career, he knew he was missing the greatest wealth, his health. At 51 years young, he suffered from high cholesterol, diabetes and debilitating sciatica. He hated being on medication but what he despised even more was not being able to stand up straight. He knew he had some runway left in his life, but he couldn't even take his daughter, whom he loved so much, shopping. The back pain was just too much to bear.

"How did this happen?" he thought to himself. Andy was always so active as a young man playing sports of all sorts. His favorites were baseball and basketball. Andy was a doer. He now played golf but was mostly sedentary. Being in the publishing business meant hours upon hours of sitting. That was bad news for the cholesterol, diabetes, and back pain.

As Hanukah was approaching, his wife, Pam, asked him what type of gift he would like. Andy knew he didn't need any more golf clubs. What he needed was to get his life back. He wanted to get off the medication and gain freedom - freedom from the pain he felt each waking hour. He also wanted to lose the extra 30 pounds that formed a "spare tire" around his midsection. His doctor would tell him at every visit that he needed to start exercising, but Andy never took it seriously. He just humored his doc and said he would start soon, never taking any action.

Now he was fifty, though, and he started gaining a new perspective. You see, Andy's beloved father had a massive heart attack at just 55 years young. This thought had been gnawing away at Andy for over a year, when he turned 50. But now he was 51. Just 4 years younger than his dad was. Andy's mortality was now a reality for him. Up to this point he was in denial. He now knew the path he was headed, and it wasn't good. His health was more similar to his dad's at that point than he would've liked to admit as they had similar habits and the same DNA.

So Andy told Pam what he really wanted. He wanted to get in shape. He had tried a few other gyms over the years, but he knew that it doesn't work if you don't go. He needed to find a different place, a place where he could fit in and want to keep going.

Pam was now on a mission to find the right solution for her husband. The first place she contacted never returned her call. Thank God! We connected right away and set up an initial meeting with Andy which we call a *Success in Fitness* Strategy Session.

I met with Andy, and we began the process of trying to get from where he was to where he wanted to be. It was a bit of a slow process at first, but this is not a bad thing. Many people overestimate how fast they will see results and set themselves up for failure. Andy understood this was a process. He was interested in the long game. With that said, he had his work cut out. We had to work on years of unproductive behaviors.

While Andy was being consistent with his workouts the first few months, I knew we had to improve his nutrition if we really wanted to ramp up his progress. As coincidence would have it (or not), I had recently had my own health scare. I was diagnosed with diabetes and for one full week, I believed I had this bully of a disease. It turned out to be a mistake, which is a different story for a different day, but this experience helped me to understand what many people are actually going through. Unfortunately for them, their diagnosis is not a mistake.

Andy pointed this out to me during a training session. He said, "Now you know how many of your clients feel." Neither Andy nor I believe in coincidences. We agree that the reason I was falsely diagnosed with diabetes was to create empathy and an understanding that I could not have gained otherwise.

As a little time passed, Andy's comment weighed on me. I knew I could help him if he was willing to help himself. I'll never forget the conversation we had on that Thursday afternoon. I told Andy that I believed I could help him get his life back. I told him I think that we could get him off the diabetes, and possibly the cholesterol medication. I didn't hide the brutal facts. It would be hard work. If Andy wanted to experience health that few people experience, he'd have to make some changes few people are willing to make. I knew he could do it, but I had to see that he was willing to trust the process and make the necessary sacrifices. Since he was going away on vacation, I knew that nutritional changes were probably not on his agenda.

I told him to think long and hard about whether he was ready to really commit to the nutritional component. Andy was always a doer and now, because of his health, he was limited in how much he could do. I knew that if Andy's perceived pain was great enough, he would be willing to endure the pain of change.

I was clear with Andy that I needed him to be committed. He had to decide on what he wanted. I explained that the Latin of the word 'decision' literally means to "cut off." He was to be focused on this area. He didn't have to be perfect. Nobody is. He just had to be committed to doing the best he could. I honestly didn't know what Andy would decide. I thought it was a good sign that he was fed up with his circumstances. Some people need to hit rock bottom before they change. I also thought it was a plus that he wanted to think about it before deciding. Sometimes when people rush into things, they go too fast, too soon, and can't sustain their new behavior.

The day Andy got back from vacation, I received this message from him:

"Hi Bill. It means a lot that you have my back. I've been thinking about your offer you made before I left for vacation. If it still stands, I would love to take you up on it. I am ready to commit."

My response:

"Andy! Absolutely. I appreciate that you took your time to make sure you were fully on board. Change is never easy but I promise it will be worth it. Stay tuned for some preliminary steps. Follow what I say, trust the process and great things will happen. No reason why you can't achieve optimal health!"

After talking further with Andy, I discovered he consulted with his doctor and his wife. Both were on board and prepared to support him. Andy mentioned that he felt like he may never get an opportunity like this again and he wanted to capitalize.

Now that I knew he was on board, we got to work. I created a plan for Andy that included education, action steps, and perhaps most important, accountability.

Little by little Andy started making changes. Before starting the plan, Andy's diet consisted of lots carbohydrates, and I'm not talking about oatmeal and quinoa. I am talking about the processed kind - the kind that can destroy your health if consumed in excess. Little by little, Andy minimized how much of these ineffective foods he ate. We certainly didn't want Andy to starve so we replaced the processed carbs with healthier ones like vegetables. We also introduced healthy fats such as nuts and avocado. Andy also drank wine and other alcoholic beverages regularly before starting the program. I explained how this behavior could wreak havoc on both body fat and perhaps more importantly the diabetes. We agreed that Andy could still have an occasional drink but it would have to be the exception rather than the rule.

Andy began to amaze me, his doctor, wife, and even himself. His doctor said it was "remarkable" how much his blood sugar came down in such a short period of time. He started building momentum as he systematically replaced unproductive habits with positive ones. He started feeling better almost immediately. Next, his clothes started feeling better and soon people started noticing. He was transforming right before us, and it was truly awesome to see. His blood sugar began to normalize now that he was eating in a manner that supported good health.

Fast forward almost 2 years now and Andy is down 30 pounds, hasn't had Taco Bell since he made the decision to change, and is off the majority of the medication he had been taking. While his back occasionally gets tight, he no longer has to put his life on hold because now he is pain free!

He looks better, feels better, and most importantly is now LIVING life. That's what life is meant for anyway, right? LIVING! He's as active as he wants to be now. He is stronger and can keep up with his kids. In fact, he now helps out other newbies that come to our facility. So, he went from being overweight, highly medicated, and in constant pain to being slim, healthy, and happy!

Andy's initial transformation was amazing, but the fact that he is maintaining his healthy lifestyle is even more impressive. Since he's started, life has happened to Andy. He suffered a shoulder injury and is helping care for his ailing mother. Andy really appreciated how we were able to tailor a specific program for him based on his unique circumstances. Many facilities take a "cookie cutter" approach but Andy was encouraged when he was able to modify his program based on his situation. Since he began, the only times I haven't seen Andy at his normal training sessions were when he was sick or out of town. "The only downside," Andy said, "is not having any clothes that fit!"

I asked Andy how he stays so focused. He told me he ignores the idea of failure. It's not an option for him. He only thinks of the positive result, not the negative of giving up. Rather than thinking how hard it is going to be to get up and go to the gym, he thinks how great he will feel after a great workout.

Another aspect that Andy pointed out was that the program worked because it was fun – Not necessarily in a Rah-Rah sort of way but he enjoys the coaches as well as the other members. It's like a second family to him and for that reason, he looks forward to each training session.

Andy has changed his life and because of it, his family, friends, and world around him are all better off. This is one person's story of triumph over health problems and pain. We all have a story. The thoughts and actions we take each day will determine where our story leads. I look forward to hearing your amazing story one day.

Billy Hofacker and Andrew Sherman

ABOUT BILLY HOFACKER

Billy Hofacker has worked with hundreds of clients helping them get fit, tone up, and feel better about themselves. A 20-year veteran of the fitness industry, he owns and operates Total Body Boot Camp and Performance Center, which has locations in Farmingdale and Babylon, NY. Billy is the author of *Lose Weight and Feel Great* as well as a contributing author to *Fuel Your Soul*. Billy is considered a thought leader, especially in the areas of habit and behavior change, nutrition coaching and corporate wellness.

Outside of his passion for helping busy people lose weight, Billy is a black belt in Brazilian Jiu-jitsu and is active in his local church. Billy and his wife Melissa live on Long Island NY with their two daughters.

To contact Billy, or book a Free No Obligation *Success in Fitness* Strategy session, *visit www.lifitnessbootcamp.com*

~~32 b calibration tube, or bought rather placed to~~

Fitness Does Not Just Transform Your Body, It Transforms Your Soul

by Tom Jackobs

I was never into fitness. I was much more comfortable tinkering with photography or in front of a computer. I also didn't think I needed fitness in my life. I was a skinny kid my entire life and couldn't gain weight even if I tried. I guess I was active enough, or at least ate the right things, to avoid putting on a lot of fat. Or maybe I was just "lucky."

When I graduated college, I weighed about 125 pounds at 5'8" tall with a twenty-nine inch waist. Clothes just hung on me as if I were a coat hanger. Then it got to me. I had pretty low self-esteem. I really wanted to "bulk up." I didn't want to be the scrawny kid anymore.

So, I began to read all I could about weight lifting and adding muscle. I bought endless amounts of supplements, simply from the pictures in the ads. Plus, I started working out.

The day after my first workout session, I could not walk. I was so sore, but I was committed. I wanted to put on weight, and I wanted to do it fast. I knew that being bigger I would feel so much more confident with myself. As a skinny kid I felt vulnerable, like I would be the last one to get a date or the first one to get beaten up. Slowly, it began to work. After 5 years, I was up to 150 pounds and had a few hard-earned muscles.

Then I stopped. My job got in the way. I did not "feel" like eating right. I wanted what was easy. I got complacent.

This is a story I see all the time at my facility. People start a program with great intentions but fall off. Life gets in the way. They lose focus. There are a million excuses. I am not immune to it either.

In the meantime, I put on 50 pounds in 6 months. "Really?!" I thought. "It took five years to put on 25 pounds of muscle, but only 6 months to put on 50 pounds of fat! What the heck!"

Unfortunately, I was committed, to *not* doing what I needed to for my health. I just couldn't make the time for exercise. I was commuting two hours a day and my sedentary life was much more comfortable than actually picking up some weights or eating right. In fact, each morning I would drive through Dunkin' Donuts, order a blueberry donut (to get my fruit for the day) and a chocolate glazed (a reward for having the fruit) and a medium coffee. It was $2.01. I always had exact change, after a week of this, the lovely donut lady, Gabby, had my order ready for me when she saw my car come around at 5am.

At lunch, I would half-ass it at the gym at work, wondering why I was gaining fat. My thought was that I needed to get some other supplements to help that out.

Before my one-and-a-half hour commute home through rush hour traffic in Chicago, I would stop off at Wendy's and get a spicy chicken sandwich (fried, of course - but it was chicken so kind of healthy) along with fries and a coke, biggie size of course. Go big or go home!

Once I got home and had my sugar crash... geez why was I so tired all the time? I'd sit on the coach in front of the television with a nice big bowl of ice cream. No wonder I had high blood pressure and high cholesterol and was 50 pounds overweight.

The trigger came when a portly co-worker saw me in the lunch room and asked if I had put on some weight because my pants were pretty tight. "I am sorry. What did you just call me?" I thought. I knew I had to do something that night. So I bought bigger pants, size 35. Ouch, I had grown from a 29 to a 35.

I was committed to finally doing something about this big problem and big gut! Buying bigger pants was just masking the real problem. The truth sometimes hurts, but it will set us free from a lifetime of health problems and early death. When I moved to Houston I was in the worst shape of my life, and my health was seriously in jeopardy. My blood pressure was skyrocketing and my cholesterol was out of control. I did not want to die early, and I certainly did not want to be a burden to others with preventable health problems.

When I moved to Houston that year I purchased the book, **_Body For Life_**, by Bill Phillips and followed it religiously. In 12 weeks, I lost 40 pounds of fat and gained 10 pounds of muscle, and I got my health back. My cholesterol was the lowest in years, and my blood pressure was perfect.

More importantly, I found my purpose.

I did not want others to go through what I did, to have to guess at what to do, to trust all of the crap that is on the internet. I wanted to offer people sound advice and a practical way of accomplishing their goals, in a safe private place, free of attitude and judgement.

That is when I opened Body3 Personal Fitness in Houston. I have the pleasure of helping clients like Sandra O'Neal, who decided to get back into fitness. Her story of transforming her body and her soul parallels my own story and struggle to stay committed. It also resonates with every single one of the thousands of Houston residents we have helped since 2008.

Here is what Sandra said about her experience and transformation.

I have had periods in my life where I was very active and healthy. However, as I settled into a career and marriage, exercise became sporadic. Ten years passed and I gained close to 100 pounds. I was miserable and unhappy. In 2009, I lost over 107 pounds and was determined to change my life. That worked for a while, but I never made the real changes I needed to make. Since then a few pounds had crept back, but I could not find the motivation to take it off and become active again.

My first introduction to Body3 was through my son and daughter-in-law. I was intrigued and envious of their excitement when talking about their 'gym' and the staff. They spoke of everyone as if they were personal friends. Over the years, I paid for several gym memberships, but never felt that kind of excitement or connection and usually stopped attending after a few weeks. Not one person from any of those gyms ever contacted me when I missed or stopped going.

So, one of the first things I did was meet with Cassandra. She explained the Body3 program and family environment. I was excited and a little scared about joining Body3. Body3 is the first place where after 6 months; I still look forward to going every day. From day one, I felt welcomed and part of a team/family whose focus was to help me improve my health, body shape and strength. When I doubt myself, they do not.

My family has noticed the changes in me and can't believe how much I love working out (actually, neither can I). My strength and flexibility continue to improve and I feel great every day. Laughter is as much a part of the Body3 workout as weight training, cardio, stretching, and foam rolling. Maybe that is the secret ingredient. All I know is without my Body3 friends/family's encouragement; I would still be sitting on the couch.

Sandra is not alone. I have seen a huge shift in what people are looking for in a fitness program. It is more than just the workouts. You can work-out anywhere and anytime, but it is rare to find a community of people who share similar values and similar goals. When the place you exercise becomes your "happy place" and is filled with friends you cannot wait to see, you start to build a healthy lifestyle. That is the kind of lifestyle which will support you as you get older.

About Tom Jackobs

Tom Jackobs, CPT RES
Certified Personal Trainer,
Rehab Exercise Specialist
Nutrition Counselor,
Author and Motivational Speaker

Having spent 12 years in the corporate world Tom made the decision to change careers into health and fitness. His company, Body3 Personal Fitness in Houston Texas offers programs which help individuals take control of their health and fitness through personalized exercise programs and nutrition programs.

Body3 Personal Fitness has been in operation since 2008 and has helped 2654 Houston residents reach their fitness goals.

In addition to running his fitness businesses, Tom is passionate about helping other entrepreneurs move from being business operators to business owners. He has traveled the globe speaking in front of thousands of fitness professionals and motivating his audiences to take control of their business and grow beyond just a job.

He has created an educational platform for entrepreneurs called "How To Be a Business Owner", teaching would be entrepreneurs how to stay in the game for the long haul, while also maintaining a lifestyle of health and happiness.

Mr. Jackobs also wrote the book on beginning an exercise program entitled **Get Off Your Butt and Do Something**, which is available at Amazon.com

To find out more about how Body3 Personal Fitness can help you, please request a consultation at <u>www.Body3Fit.com/fitnessconsult</u> or call 713-864-1231

FROM HELL TO HAPPINESS: THE UNTOLD SECRETS OF A JOURNEY CALLED LIFE

By Sean Lee

Hi. My name is Sean Lee. I have been training bodies and transforming minds for the better part of two decades. I have countless transformations I could share, but none quite like this. If you like stories of overcoming the impossible, you are going to love this!

Allison and I first connected in the fall of 2015. She was 56 at the time and newly married. This southern bell was in all-out marriage bliss. She finally rediscovered what it was like to be happy again. The pain and emptiness that imprisoned her for so long was gone, or so she thought.

Hold on tight, more on that in a minute.

Allison was nearing the end of a brutal, three-year divorce. It was an unbelievably difficult time. Allison felt she could never live up to his expectations. No matter what she did he could do it better. The emotional drain crushed her self-confidence, and left her depressed and empty.

Allison was quite the social butterfly. Oh, yes - everyone knew her. Her southern charm and infectious smile lit up a room. Until the divorce.

The emotional scars were being laid, one by one. Happiness quickly turned to anger, frustration, and fear. On the outside she stayed strong. On the inside... emotional turmoil.

Like many of us, during stressful times Allison turned to food for comfort and control. One of Allison's greatest fears was being alone. This stemmed from her childhood. When she was born, she enjoyed the time and attention her parents gave her as the only child. At the age of 4 her sister was born and a year later, the twins. Her parents' focus had to quickly shift from Allison to the 3 newborns.

I remember when she first shared this with me. Allison said, "when I was 10, I baked my first batch of chocolate chip cookies. The aroma was like kryptonite. One bite into the warm gooey center of that first cookie and I was hooked." It filled a void. She now found companionship in food.

With the divorce in full swing, panic set in. She was alone again. But the human brain is an amazing thing. There was already a safety mechanism in place. Baking those sweet southern treats would rescue her when she needed them most. Baking was exactly what she needed to gain emotional stability.

It didn't end there. Allison used her love for baking, not only as a coping strategy during the divorce, but as a way to express her love to her new hubby. For years she baked her infamous pies, cookies, and cakes. And for years she indulged in these delightful treats.

As Allison settled into her new life she found herself without friends. Her husband worked full time. Allison dabbled in some part time work ventures, but nothing she truly enjoyed.

This brought Allison back to a familiar place. Although married and completely fulfilled in her relationship, she once again, found herself alone. But this wasn't Allison's only problem.

Unknowingly, her health had been on a steady decline for years dating back to the divorce. Now it had spun completely out of control. A routine physical confirmed she was pre-diabetic. She was also put on medications to manage depression, and cholesterol. Like most doctors in this situation, he recommended she start eating right and exercising.

Allison had no choice. She had to do something. She was the heaviest she had ever been. Her clothes didn't fit. A trip to the closet was like a walk thru hell. The cravings were uncontrollable and holding her hostage. The joint pain was terrible. So bad she started anti-inflammatories just to get through the day.

Food had been a loving and caring friend for so long. A source of companionship and comfort. But now what? Allison was trapped in a body she couldn't escape.

Determined to regain control of her life she was willing to try anything. And she did. Each attempt an epic failure.

Her spirit, broken and more confused than ever, she grew fearful of what the future would hold. Would she be around to enjoy life with her new hubby, see her kids get married, grandchildren born? This emotional rollercoaster put her into a state of complete and total desperation.

About that time she came across our ad for a 21-Day challenge fitness and nutrition program. Intrigued, she decided to come in for a consultation.

In our meeting she said, "*Sean I am desperate. I don't know if you can help me. I've tried everything and nothing has worked. I'm so frustrated! My doctor told me I am pre-diabetic and I need to do something now! I am*

110

hungry all the time, I don't sleep, and have these uncontrollable cravings. I am willing to try anything."

I said, "Allison I can help you. I know we just met, but I am asking for your trust. I promise together we can change your life."

Below is an email I received from her after her first week on the program…

"I just have to stop and tell you this nutrition/exercise program is really working for me! It's only been a week and my cravings for sweets and wine are gone – honestly, I never would have believed it would happen to me. I have more energy later in the afternoon and evening then I've ever had before. I haven't felt stuffed like I usually do and my clothes are looser which is hard to believe after only a week. Thanks so much for what you have put together at RF – for the first time in my life, I'm beginning to believe that this is a lifestyle change that will last, not just another diet and exercise program".

Her transformation was in full swing.

Now is a good time to point out that Allison started changing on the inside first. Her emotional metabolism was nurtured through our meetings and social interaction with other members of the studio. The bond we formed, and friends she made is where the healing started. This had to take place before a physical transformation was possible.

She wasn't alone. She was immersed into a community of people who genuinely cared for her. As a result, Allison lost 28 pounds and 16 inches in 6-months. She was happier then she had ever been. Her tight cloths were loose. Her joint pain gone. She was no longer pre-diabetic and the medications managing her depression and cholesterol were no longer necessary.

She was a new woman. Allison was so moved by her transformation, she joined our team in the fall of 2015 to support others, like her, who so badly want to change their lives.

Her energy and smile breathe life into our business every day. She inspires change and truly has found her passion.

I hope this inspires you to take action with confidence that change is possible at any age, or stage of life.

We all have emotional scars that hold us back from what we really want. Identifying yours, with the right support, tools, and system, is the key to unlocking the happiness that lies with-in.

Sound crazy? Hardly. Just ask Allison. She is a believer. Are you?

ABOUT SEAN LEE

Sean is a speaker, author, and personal trainer with more than two decades of experience in the health and fitness industry. His passion is helping people like you transform your life from the inside out. It's what gets him is out of bed everyday excited to make a difference in the world.

He is a Certified Personal Trainer and Corrective Exercise Specialist through the National Academy of Sports Medicine; a Certified Personal Trainer through the American Council on Exercise; and a Certified Strength and Conditioning Specialist through the National Strength and Conditioning Association; and a Mindset Performance Specialist thru the Mindset Performance Institute.

His life changing philosophy combines the art and science of Mindset, Nutrition, Exercise, Accountability, and Coaching. He understands you need a better solution. A complete lifestyle approach.

Sean believes to make sustainable changes in our health we first must rewire what's between our ears. The mind chatter we all experience controls everything from what we think to how we act. These patterns become our actions, habits, and results.

No matter what your goal may be – weight loss, muscle tone, better energy, or anything between, with the right tools and support, you to can change your life. You deserve to live a healthier and more fulfilling life. A life without limits. A life that allows you to do the things you love for as long as you want to do them. A life that brings happiness and fulfillment.

Sean is the CFO (Chief Fitness Officer) and owner of Restoration Fitness a personal training studio located in Lake Zurich, IL. For more information, go to www.restorationfitness.com

MY DAY TO DAY STRUGGLE

by Arin and Tony Lindauer

The Struggle

Day after day Debbie would get up with aches and pains. Sometimes the pain was more than she could bear.

This is normal, right?

After all she was 62, she had back issues (Degenerative Discs, arthritis, spondylolisthesis), sciatic pain, her A1C (sugar level) was too high putting her at risk for Type 2 Diabetes, taking multiple high blood pressure medicines and had Stage 4 Kidney Disease.

Debbie said, "She hated herself and felt like she was getting worse and worse." She felt like one thing kept compounding to the next. Debbie also said, "I could just continue living life like this...or I could do something about it."

Debbie is your classic female who always put herself last. We see women do this over and over. They are so used to taking care of everyone but themselves. For most people this is their "normal." They live with the pain and suffering from a medical condition, aging and being deconditioned. They feel working out is something those young people do, or it's too overwhelming on where to start.

But Debbie knew she needed to do something about her health. She could continue to get diagnosis after diagnosis, this treatment, this drug, but she ultimately knew she needed to take control of her health on her terms. Ultimately there was a huge ache in her heart for why she needed to be in good health.

The Decision to Change Her Life

It was May 2016 that Debbie saw one of our emails for a challenge we were getting ready to launch. She had been through some health scares, injuries and almost felt she was too old. We exchanged a few email s and jumped on the phone. I can honestly tell you Debbie had every reason not to workout – injuries, health conditions, illnesses, finances, time. We could go on and on, but there was one little force pushing her to take care of herself.

That little tug was her Grandson.

Debbie gets to be with him every Saturday and she cherishes that time with him. She was scared she could not care for him. The biggest eye opener for her was she could not carry him up the stairs at 6 weeks old. This tugged at her heart and again pushed her forward.

There is always a reason we take those first scary steps when joining a new program to better our life. Something is pulling at our heart strings and the pain of staying the same is too much. We draw that line in the sand and make that decision that from this day forward, "I need to be different."

For Debbie it was her grandson. Ask yourself…what's pulling at you? What do you wish you could do? What is causing the pain or hurt in your life? Are you ready to do something about it?

Everything is going great until…

We would love to tell you everything goes smoothly when you make the decision to change your life.

HA…that's when it gets the hardest.

The aches and pains don't just magically go away. Weight loss doesn't just happen because you purchased a fancy gym membership. Changing your life is hard work and, typically, it's more work than most people are willing to do.

If I can be brutally honest here - most people quit just when they would have turned the corner. It gets too hard, life gets in the way, time, money, and so on.

For Debbie, it was no different. She was terminated from job of 27 years, 3 months into her transformation. Could she have given up? Yes, you bet, and I would not have blamed her! She had no clue how she was going to pay for her gym membership, let alone her house payment.

Then to top it all off she received a diagnosis that had the potential be cancerous. Just let that sink in. All the sudden you start to do amazing things in your life. Debbie was down about 30 pounds at this point. She was starting to get in a really great routine. Then, out of nowhere, life just attacks.

But Debbie would not give up. She figured it out. She sold her house, began consulting some clients on her own, found another job and did not give up on her weight loss journey. Then because everything happens in three's, or at least it seems that way, Debbie got in a car accident that totaled her car. Thankfully she was ok, but the car was not.

Here she was, facing hit after hit -her job of 27 years, major health scare and now totaling her car. But she did not quit. She figured it out. Every

Saturday she got to see her "why" - her grandson. Because of him, she pushed forward.

New Year's Resolution

Debbie was getting close to 200 pounds for the first time and she made it a goal to achieve this by the end of the year. The workouts were hard, and the nutrition was even harder. We helped her feel comfortable and successful in the workouts and gave her modifications that were appropriate for her.

Even though our workouts are in a group (Team) setting, the workout is your personal workout. We can modify any movement. She said she hurt most workouts, I could even see the pain in her eyes, but she always pushed through. (Appropriately) Talk about grit. You either have it or you don't. Debbie has grit. She looks for how she can do anything versus looking at all the things she can't do. She never made excuses.

That's a huge lesson for all of us. We tend to always focus on the negative. Just listen to the people around you. When faced with adversity, do you just cave and give up or do you look for solutions?

At this point, Debbie was making huge strides in her workout program. She set an awesome goal to be less than 200 pounds by the end of the year. This was only seven months after starting our program, and it would put her at a total of 55 pounds gone!

We were so happy to hear in Debbie's assessment 2 days before the New Year. She had achieved her goal and then some!

When you are on your weight loss journey with us it is personal. We take your successes and struggles to heart. Seeing Debbie's success in just seven short months was simply amazing, after 2016 being a year of so many struggles, she still persevered.

118

How Do You Keep Pushing Forward?

Debbie will tell you she is a work in progress. She said, "I want to be a normal size sometime in my life, which I have never been."

We are so proud to tell you Debbie has lost 82 pounds from her body in only 10 months and she is still going! When I asked Debbie how she feels, she lit up. She experiences a pride in herself she never knew was possible. She is not only proud of her results, but that she stuck with it. Also, she can move so much better. She said she is not pain free but it is so much better than it was.

In our program, we believe nutrition is 70-80% of everyone's results. Debbie will tell you she approaches food differently than before. She understands portion sizes, what foods have sugar in them, and she also understood that she had to be consistent with her nutrition habits. This is where we see most clients struggle.

Debbie has always appreciated our approach. She knew she had a long way to go with her health, but we helped her break it down into bite size pieces. We had her set goals in six week increments. Six weeks is long enough to see results, and it is obtainable. Then we would reassess and set new goals for another six-week period.

When someone is thinking about a year of work, or a big scary number on the scale, it can be overwhelming. Breaking down the goal helps make the goal more obtainable.

We captured a picture every six weeks. Even though Debbie had great assessments she could still get down on herself, but when you showed her the starting picture, compared to the 'now' picture, that was all she needed to keep forging forward.

I asked Debbie, "How are you different now than when you first started this transformation?"

119

She replied, "I never would have shared this story. I am the type of person that stays in the background and I never want to stand out." Debbie also said that she feels it is important to share and to be a leader! She talked about how the other members in her workouts would congratulate her and say she is an inspiration.

Another amazing difference Debbie talked about was getting off medicines. She was able to get completely off one medicine for blood pressure and reduce another by half! She is so excited to get bloodwork done again, one year later! We know those numbers are going to be amazing. This is one of the coolest things that happen when people start taking care of themselves. Not only the weight on the scale, but the amount of pride they feel when they no longer have to depend on a drug.

Debbie said she did not feel she could do this alone, but with help and guidance from our Fitness Professionals and the encouragement from the others in class, it has made all the difference. She never wanted to have a personal trainer one-on-one. She said that would draw too much attention to her, but that she likes the small group or team atmosphere.

She originally had a fear of going to the gym and not fitting in. She also felt everyone had muscles and knew what they were doing. At our gym, she feels welcomed and is encouraged by others working out. We workout in a team, you are not alone and everyone has common goals.

Debbie offers one more piece of advice by encouraging others to take that scary first step through our doors. Once you are inside, we will take care of the rest. Taking that first step is the hardest part, but you will never look back.

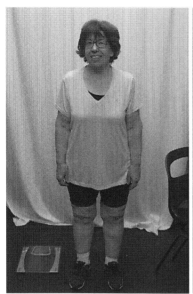

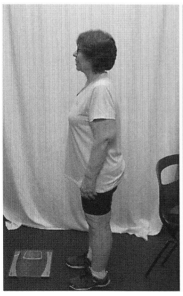

ABOUT ARIN AND TONY LINDAUER

Arin and Tony Lindauer, owners of Transformation Fitness and Wellness, a Team Training Facility, are leading providers of preventative health care in the Indianapolis market.

They have transformed thousands of lives utilizing fitness and wellness strategies and continue to develop cutting- edge programs to address the growing healthcare crises. They have staffed qualified Fitness Professionals - who they continue to develop professionally and personally to change even more lives.

When Arin realized how she could change people's lives by motivating them, she sought out a Bachelor of Science degree in Exercise Science. When she received her first success story of a client no longer relying on arthritis medicine, she was hooked! Tony understood the science behind fitness and wellness because of his Masters of Science in Biomechanics, and became an advocate to educate clients on how to get the most out of their fitness. He has a passion to encourage all clients to challenge their bodies and take the tools from him and use them in their everyday life. One ex-ample was that of a gentleman who came in to Transformation Fitness and Wellness because of the extreme back pain that caused him the inability to stand up straight. Tony, who understands the value of living pain-free, was able to help the gentleman. In a matter of months, Tony had helped him strengthen his body, stretch properly, and now he walks everyday pain-free with improved posture!

With the growing 'epidemic' of unhealthy Americans, Arin and Tony are devoted to developing educated fitness and wellness solutions for all clients. When a person emails, calls, or walks through their door, they know they are going to be treated with integrity and a standard of care like no other. The Fitness Professionals at Trans-formation Fitness and Wellness must be educated, maintain a standard of personal health, and they continue to develop themselves to provide 'best care' for each client. The compassion they have when they see the physical and emotional pain of a client, instantly makes them want to help alleviate that pain.

Arin, Tony and their staff are in the business of changing lives. They continue to do this every day and get the most gratification from their clients' testimonials. Each testimonial is another life changed forever. Come be transformed and be their next testimonial!

Contact:

Transformation Fitness and Wellness
www.tfwellness.com
support@tfwellness.com
317-927-9689

I Don't Know
if I am Fixable

by Brad Linder

I have been a Transformation Expert since 1999, and my initial meeting with JoAnn stands out as one of the most memorable moments I have ever had. She came to me at her darkest hour.

It was early March 2016, and JoAnn signed up, at the last minute, for our **Get You In Shape** Group Nutrition Challenge. After the kickoff meeting, she came up to me and shared what she was going through.

At age 52, JoAnn began to cry as she explained she was sleeping most of her life away. She was depressed, had no energy, was in the worst shape of her life, was bursting out of her clothes, and had lost hope. Having a strong desire to help her, I asked her to share a little more of her backstory so I could serve her better.

I Didn't Think This Could Happen to Me

JoAnn shared that her chauffeuring days as a mother of two children were over. Her household was now staying up and eating later so her clock adjusted accordingly. Instead of seizing the day, she was wasting hours on the computer or staying in bed. Her husband, Mike, would kiss her goodbye as he left for work, but she would stay in bed until noon.

For a long time, JoAnn thought it was selfish to do an exercise program while her husband worked long hours. It seemed unfair and costly. She was relieved to hear he wanted her to start a fitness program. Mike knew she was miserable and could not do it on her own. She tried two smelly gyms and two personal trainers with no success.

Then four months before this March evening, she participated in our Thanksgiving Charity Workout to help a local food bank. She explained the workout was fun, challenging, and manageable. However, she thought she should get in shape <u>before</u> joining **Get You In Shape** (GYIS).

It took several more painful months for her to finally take the step and make it to this meeting where she agonized,

> *"I didn't see this happening to me. I was fit in my twenties and thirties, but now I am scared. I am scared that if I continue to neglect my health, I will hit the 200 pound mark and never regain a recognizable me. I can no longer wear my wedding ring because I'm too big for it to fit. I can't be in any more family pictures because I am so big.*
>
> *I recently took my teenage son and young grandson to the neighborhood trampoline park and just watched. Jumping for me is tiring, and I was certain I looked foolish.*
>
> *Still the scariest part is feeling like I will lose my life. My dear husband loves me so much, and he might die of a broken heart [if anything happened to me]. I know I need help, and I know I'm finally ready.*
>
> *So I got dressed and cried my way over to this meeting. I don't know if I am fixable but I trust you and am ready to start now."*

You Are Fixable

It is moments like this when I am grateful for the opportunity to have a positive impact on someone's life. I could tell JoAnn was at the point where she was miserable and feared for her life if she didn't do something about it now. I assured her I could help her. She was fixable, and all she needed to do was "follow the darn instructions."

JoAnn committed herself to our program for 12 months that night, and I committed to helping her feel alive and happy again. She later mentioned when she heard the words "you are fixable," they were the ray of hope she was looking for and the proof she needed to get started right then and there.

SO THAT... I Can Be with my Loved Ones

After the initial meeting, the first thing JoAnn and I did was define goals and reasons **WHY** she wanted to achieve them. We all want to lose weight, get healthy, and have more energy. It is the reason WHY that allow us to make the right choices each and every day. We call these motives "SO THAT'S."

JoAnn's WHY was "SO THAT... I can be with my loved ones."

I asked her to write this message on a 3 x 5 card and carry it with her throughout the day. Having this visual helped her make smarter choices. She was making her choices SO THAT she could be with her loved ones.

Follow the Darn Instructions

The next thing we did was create JoAnn's step-by-step "follow the darn instructions" plan which included the three keys to both short-term results and the lifestyle she desired long term: accountability, consistent exercise, and following our nutrition system. Our GYIS Group Nutrition Challenge incorporates all of these elements so we got her started right away!

I utilized several ways to keep JoAnn accountable. First I matched her up with one of our GYIS Accountability Coaches to walk along the journey with her so she did not feel alone. We provided a positive fitness environment where she felt welcomed from the moment she started. Our community rallied around her and motivated her to show up to workout sessions each and every week.

My team and I taught her how to track her daily calories with a special app we use which has been proven to maximize results. Tracking her calories daily allowed JoAnn to answer to herself. We also held her accountable with weigh-ins and measurements every two weeks throughout the year.

Consistent exercise with the Get You In Shape fitness program was also vital to JoAnn's transformation. We provide group personal training sessions with flexible schedules so there are no excuses for not showing up.

At her first follow up meeting just a week after starting, I could already notice a difference in her mood. She had also lost some inches and weight.

GYIS hosts monthly 5ks so our fitness family can come together in a non-competitive environment and support each other through a long run. It took JoAnn 53 years to run her first 5k, which she did on her birthday with her son just one month after joining our program (Note: With GYIS friends, she now has a passion for running races).

After the first month, JoAnn lost 10 pounds. It is funny how when you are ready for a change, change happens. By month three, she was down 25 pounds.

In addition to consistent workouts, JoAnn would be the first to tell you that a healthy diet and following our Nutritional System was critical to achieving her goals. Learning to eat well-balanced meals and adding nutritional supplements to her day was a journey.

She had to eventually gut her refrigerator and recently shared she has only purchased one box of cereal all year. She is cooking organic meals most of the time and adds healthy shakes and bars from our nutrition line when she is crunched for time.

Happy People Sing

I asked JoAnn in her own words to share what has taken place since that dark night ten months ago:

> *"Today I am 40 pounds lighter. My wedding rings fit again! My husband and I celebrated our anniversary in the Caymans and walked 20,000 steps every day. It was the best vacation ever!*
>
> *In under a year, working this program has made me feel and look ten years younger. I have dropped more than three pant sizes, and I can wear a swimsuit outside of my backyard and proudly sport a bikini on the beach.*
>
> *My new self goes beyond what you see! My new self includes better choices for my family and myself. We choose activities which require moving. I went from watching*

my grandson jump at the trampoline park to jumping with him... from never running a 5k to running my first one with my son and now preparing for a half marathon.

I make more attempts at going to bed earlier and starting the day earlier, tracking my food, exercising, and appreciating the Gift of Each Day.

My life has changed! In fact, I even joined our community chorale because I am happy, and happy people sing."

Life is Great

I am grateful JoAnn trusted me to help her with this journey. By providing her with a positive environment, I witnessed her transformation from being hopeless to feeling alive again.

She followed the GYIS "darn instructions" and was held accountable by herself, coach, and fitness family as well as exercised more and used the Nutrition System.

JoAnn's now paying it forward by sharing her testimony and lifting our community with hope. She went from her darkest night to spreading sunshine.

"Energy is life, and with all the new energy I have found through Get You in Shape, my life is great!" she says.

Thanks to JoAnn, I have found a new sense of purpose and passion in what I am doing. I now understand, more than ever, that we are all striving to be the best version of ourselves. I feel humbled to be a part of the fixing process.

Brad Lnder and JoAnn Talkington

ABOUT BRAD LINDER

As a former professional basketball player, Brad utilized the knowledge attained from a Master's degree in Health, Kinesiology, and Sport Studies to optimize his performance. With an extensive background in fitness and nutrition, he naturally wanted to share this knowledge with others as he entered into the health and fitness field.

Since 1999, Brad has been able to help 2,463 people get in the best shape of their lives. 475 of these clients are featured in video testimonies on YouTube (http://bit.ly/2mXP60Q)

In 2006, Brad founded Get You In Shape (GYIS) based in Coppell, Texas. GYIS provides scientific based, no-hype health and fitness solutions by delivering outstanding health and fitness experiences.

Brad has pioneered a high intensity group personal training program called the Get You In Shape Fitness program, which has received rave reviews including a feature in The Obama Diaries, by Laura Ingraham.

It's grown into one of the leading fitness companies in Dallas and was featured on *The Doctor's television* show with Jillian Michaels as being one of the Top Fitness Companies in Texas.

Brad has also created and produced the Get You In Shape DVD. He's a best-selling author and has been featured as a fitness expert in numerous newspapers and media appearances including *The Doctor's*, ABC New Channel 8, and CNN.

Brad has used his gift with fitness to lead Charity Events and give back to worthy causes in the community. To date, Get You In Shape has been raised more than $90,000 for various charities.

BE FIT FOR LIFE

by Damien Maher

At times I was embarrassed to tell this story, but if it helps you get back on track with your health, or if it helps a personal trainer see the world through different eyes it will be worth it.

Today, you might see me as a personal trainer, in relatively good physical shape, training hard lifting weights in the gym and playing soccer, but it may surprise you to learn that it hasn't always been that way.

Born in a working class area, I was led to believe I had two options in life either become successful in sport or learn a trade as a carpenter, electrician or brick-layer.

I chose sport, and it gave me an opportunity to become a professional soccer player. Back then soccer went through lean times, and it became increasingly hard to get paid to play, so I sought an apprenticeship in fitness working in a Big Box gym.

I traveled the world taking private internships with coaches of Olympic and World champions, physical therapists, osteopaths, chiropractors and rehabilitation experts. I learned many tools and skills from these mentors and rarely questioned their training methods due to their success.

In 2009, achieving great results with my clients inspired me to open Be Fit For Life Performance Centre, a 3000 sq ft custom made gym designed to transform our clients' bodies and improve performance.

Television roles in reality TV shows, best-selling author status and a national weekly columnist in an Irish newspaper were some of the trappings of my success.

A niggle in my hip that I had noticed when I was playing soccer had become more painful, and it started to aggravate, inhibiting my lower body training.

I was given the number of a specialist to get a diagnosis, but I ignored it for many months as I was frightened to know the outcome.

But eventually, the constant pain became too much to bear. My walking pattern, unknown to me but visible to others, changed to avoid pain. I made the decision to get the X-Ray, and the subsequent results showed that there was degenerative osteoarthritis in both hip joints, with a CAM type FAI (femoral acetabular impingement) and no cartilage in my left hip creating bone on bone wear and tear. My worst fears had come true.

The orthopedic surgeon took one look at my X-Rays and turned to me and said;

"Your hips have degenerative osteoarthritis, and you need a total left hip replacement."

At 37 years of age, stunned with the news, I enquired what would I be able to do after the surgery.

"You will be able to walk, swim and cycle."

"What about lifting weights or playing soccer?"

"Damien, you are entering a new stage of life, I don't recommend you do either. I can fit you in for surgery in two weeks time."

I saw my whole life's work in fitness, and my identity as a fitness expert come crashing down.

I questioned what I would do if I couldn't work in fitness? What about my gym I worked so hard to build? I cannot be an expert if I can't physically take part in what I recommend.

I decided to cancel the operation. Two meetings with two other surgeons provided no further answers to what patients were able to do post-surgery.

My search for hope brought me to a specialist, Professor McMinn in Birmingham, UK. His patients had made a return to sports and the gym. It gave me hope of how life could be after hip replacement surgery. This surgeon had developed a style of hip surgery that suited the younger person, who just like me was injured from sports. He would keep as much as my hip-bone intact and replace the head of my hip bone with a titanium based ball and socket.

Still not convinced I needed the operation I tried to delay it. The turning point soon came during a fitness course in Sweden. My limp had become more evident, and I felt like a lonely bystander unable to participate in the physical part of the course.

I had to stop every 20 meters of the 800-metre walk back to the hotel because each step was accompanied by a sharp excruciating pain.

Halfway there, I nearly passed out with pain as I could not walk any further or tolerate more pain. I entered a restaurant, and with tears in my eyes, I asked the waitress could she call me a Taxi to take me the last 400 meters to the hotel.

The degeneration in my hip had gone too far, and now surgery was unavoidable.

I flew alone to Birmingham, UK to face my fears and undergo the hip replacement surgery.

Not much sleep was had the night after surgery. My legs fixed in a position to prevent any movement in my new hip but I looked forward to beginning rehabilitation with my physiotherapist in the morning.

The scale of my challenge was evident on the day the physiotherapist asked me to stand up beside the bed to begin the first stages of learning how to walk again. I fainted with weakness falling to the bed.

Each day, I got a little stronger learning how to walk again with crutches. When I looked in the mirror, I was literally in tears as I realized my body had visibly wasted away. Just like everybody else, with inactivity and too much comfort food to deal with the emotional pain, I lost so much of my muscle, and I gained fat… and I visibly aged fast.

I had succumbed to Sarcopenia, the Greek word for vanishing flesh. Losing muscle reduced my metabolic rate (number of calories you burn at rest), and it increased the likelihood of fat gain and obesity. A term I refer to this as Sarco-Obesity.

In bed, at night I wondered whether I would recover and also wondering what my peers in the fitness industry, clients, and prospective clients would think about a fitness expert who has had a hip replacement. The psychological repercussions of the surgery would prove to take longer than the physical injury to recover.

I started to question my training methods and that of my mentors. How did my injury happen and what training methods worked before surgery and why and what lessons could I learn from my experience?

I designed a rehabilitation plan, applying the knowledge I had accumulated over the years to re-educate my dormant muscles how to work again, improving my connection between my mind and muscles in a system of training called isometric training. I returned to the gym to begin rehabilitation, officially the weakest person in the gym.

For nearly a month, I leaned on the support of family, co-workers and true friends as I needed help putting on my socks, getting up from the ground and also putting my leg in certain positions to train as I was physically too weak to put it there.

This increased my empathy for new clients who feel vulnerable, embarking on their fitness journey, because physically, I was a shadow of the person who had performed sports at an elite level.

I developed a new, inspiring vision for my future and transformed it into steps and stages... monthly, weekly, and daily goals focusing on progress and not perfection.

I completely changed my eating patterns, working hard in the weight room modifying each exercise to suit my limited ability. Previously, my focus was on outcomes and external performance. The increasing of weights being the goal and hitting a distance of a bar to the chest on bench press or ass to grass on squats. My recovery was based on internal performance and listening to my muscle's ability and the range of motion at my joints that my body had on that day.

I had developed an open mind in my learning. My injury inspired me to travel the world to learn from all the professions who treat injuries to ask questions and accumulate a bigger set of tools and skills to facilitate my rehabilitation and that of my more mature clients who were not being catered for in the fitness industry.

When people over forty, who spent years focusing on family, relationships and career do decide to make a commitment to their health, they receive an inadequate assessment if any and they start a one size fits all fitness program designed for the twenty-somethings.

Just as you require different clothes to fit you individually on the outside of your body, you need a bespoke custom fit solution in exercise to suit your individual anatomical differences on the inside of your body.

I decided to change our business model and expand our gym from 3000 sq ft to 6000 sq ft to match my new vision. Along with my coaches, we invested time, energy and finances to provide solutions, and purchased custom equipment for our clients who wanted to Be Fit at Forty and Beyond.

Today I can tell you this: I am more grateful for a healthy and strong body now than I EVER was before! I am delighted to be pain-free and alive. My life has changed since my surgery. I wouldn't go back and change any of it if I could because it has all been an edifying, humbling (although very embarrassing) and transformative experience. I have a new life today and a new fitness business that allows me to put my passion for fitness to work every day!

I tell my clients today what I learned painfully and personally… we all respond the same way to inactivity and over-eating. I am just like you. And you are just like me in that when you start working out and eating right, and you follow a smart plan, your body will reward you with incredible changes and renewed health!

I've been there… I know what it is like to be stuck in a body that is in pain and is not capable of doing what you want. It nearly broke my spirit, and I contemplated throwing in the towel and blaming it all on sport, exercise and the symptoms of aging. But then I decided I wasn't settling for this! I made a decision to get my body and my mind back on track.

I continue to get leaner and stronger and become a better version of myself. Each year I set a goal to look my best that year to demonstrate that hard work intelligently done in the gym improving your body can transform your life.

I look at my biggest adversity as my biggest blessing. I am grateful that I wake up every day and go to Be Fit For Life to help people overcome their challenges, transform their body shapes, avoid surgery, illness or rehabilitate from injuries and surgeries.

If you want my help rebuilding your body for life, come work with me at my fitness center in Dublin. We have different programs where I share what I know and help you get inspired to transform as I have done myself. Be Fit For Life is the best investment you will ever make in your health. If you want my help, email me at info@befitforlife.ie.

Recovery

Post-Recovery

About Damien Maher

Damien Maher is the founder of Be Fit For Life, a series of upscale training facilities designed to change lives and help people Be Fit at forty and beyond. A best-selling author, former professional footballer, and international speaker with over twenty years of experience, he is on his way to becoming one of the world's leading high performance coaches bringing peak health to some of Irelands and the UK's leading CEO'S and business leaders which allows them to improve their bottom line.

When he speaks, people listen, minds become inspired and people are motivated into action, with his enlightening perspectives and practical action steps. His revolutionary understanding of human behaviors, exercise science and rehabilitation is reshaping the personal training and fitness coaching industry.

UNDENIABLY UNSTOPPABLE

by Linda Mallard

This is a story about a young woman who has more grit, tenacity, courage and strength than anyone I have yet to meet. She inspires me on a daily basis and serves as a reminder that nothing is too hard, to keep going, and that wonderful things in life are available to all of us.

I will briefly share Emily's journey with cancer, but not to belabor this part of her life. It is what has taken place since her remission that I really want to share with you.

In 2007 at age 21, Emily Novak was diagnosed with Acute Myelogenous Leukemia. This started a journey of treatment; recurring cancer in her brain, another series of treatments, including chemotherapy, surgeries and then body breakdown from the treatments. Her family was told on several accounts that she had only 2-8 weeks to live. The doctors clearly didn't know Emily's spirit and strength. Now they do.

Between 2011 (25 years of age) and 2012 (27 years of age), Emily received a bi-lateral shoulder replacement, bi-lateral hip replacement, and double cataract surgery. She was diagnosed by her neurologist with bi-lateral extremity weakness with foot drops. Then, one year later, in 2013, Emily was admitted to hospital with severe chest and back pain and was later diagnosed with osteoporosis in her thoracic spine. X-rays indicated compression fractures in other vertebrae including fractured ribs and cracked sternum. Emily underwent vertebroplasty surgery

142

(cement in her spine). She was told she might not walk again and would live at her current level of pain.

During this time, Emily lost her hair. It will not grow back. She was also placed on major pain medications such as methadone and dexamethasone. She participated in hospital rehabilitation and was sent home in 2013 when she could transfer herself from her wheelchair to her bed. She completed a Quick Start Program as an outpatient and then joined Pilates at The Tsawwassen Wellness Centre.

During the early stages of her diagnosis, Emily had participated in a short Pilates program at the Tsawwassen Wellness Centre. Throughout her journey with cancer, she would call us and say "*I want to come back. I know Pilates will help me.*" Each time we would review her medical condition, and then inform her that her condition was not yet in our scope of practice. We encouraged her to keep with her hospital program and told her we would be here for her when she was ready.

In 2014, with her doctor's permission, Emily and I began our journey together. Initially, our sessions included gentle mobility exercises, balance exercises, retraining of her nervous system (visual, vestibular and neuromuscular exercises) and breath work. She attended twice per week. More often than not, Emily was exhausted, in pain and not feeling well. But she showed up. She was clear, "*I won't miss this for anything. If I am to get better I have to get here.*"

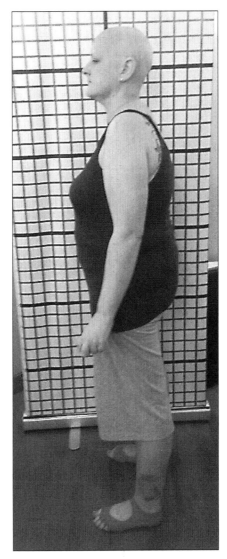

*(Emily at her first appointment
in December 2014)*

Consistency of her attendance was critical. I focused on the sessions "not being too hard." Having a positive movement experience every time we were together started to shift her paradigm of well-being. She would leave feeling more energized. Smiling and laughing connected her movements to feeling good at a cellular level. As long as Emily knew she could "do it", she would return. Sometimes we tossed a tennis ball (hand-eye coordination) or did seated exercises as lying down made her dizzy. We focused on basic foot exercises, and we tackled our sessions one body part and one joint at a time.

Some days were easier and others more challenging. It was an emotional journey as she detoxed off methadone. The nausea, pain, fatigue and depression that showed up as part of the detoxification process never stopped her. Emily knew she only had one option- *"keep moving forward, one step, one day at a time."*

There were times when Emily would say she did not want to do an exercise, but after a short pause, she would get on board and do it anyway because she knew she could. She trusted that I would only give her an exercise that I knew she could do.

Between the Pilates equipment and Emily's determination, we strengthened her legs, her core, her trunk and arms. Gait, posture, endurance and daily movements were part of our routine. Her drop foot started to improve. She was walking, standing up on her own and, over time, she was able to get herself down to the floor and up. We sang silly songs or counted really loud to distract from the fatigue. Emily would talk, tell stories and share how she was doing. She kept moving.

Within a year, Emily progressed from her Mom escorting her into the studio, to using a cane, and then walking in on her own. The entire team at the Studio rallied with her. Everyone from the staff and the clients supported her and fell in love with her.

(2015- Emily and I each in a leg of her pajama's that she wore when she was in hospital.)

Over time, Emily's energy, mobility and confidence increased, and she started participating more in life. Every doctor's appointment brought positive news. Her bone density was improving and she continues to be cancer free, with healthy blood levels.

Emily joined art classes, went out with her friends and started dating on-line. Every Tuesday we would hear about her latest date or weekend fun with friends. When a date didn't work out, she would simply say *"If that person isn't going to get back to me, then they don't deserve to be with me."* Or *"we will be ok as friends."* And then she would keep on trucking.

Emily worked one on one with me for the first year. She watched our small group classes (5 clients in a class) and asked if she could join in.

"Not yet," I'd say. *"You are getting there."* She had to be able to move herself into and out of certain positions to be safe in a Pilates class. We made a list of the things she needed to be able to do to join a class, and we did them every session.

As Emily became stronger, we checked off another success on our list. In 4 short months of setting this goal, she joined our Healthy Back class. She kept her private session once per week, but enjoyed being part of a group. Emily brought something so special with her candidness, courage and openness to share and encourage others.

For three years now, Emily continues to attend Pilates twice per week. Nothing gets in her way. I often see the look in her eyes and know she is having a hard day. I ask *"How you are today?"* She is honest with a brief share as she walks into the Studio, then she puts her water bottle down and says, *"Where are we starting?"*

In March 2016, Emily headed out for another date. She stopped trying to date for a while, but one night logged onto her Match.com account and starting chatting with a young man. They went out one night. The report back was positive at her next session. While I could see the "glimmer in her eye", she stayed 'chill' and said, *"We had fun. I'll see if he calls me back."* Well he did. They went out again, and again.

Emily found love. This man loves her for all the same reasons we do. They enjoy walks together, swimming together, and going to movies. Emily is living her life now. She is committed to her program of Pilates and art classes and on March 12, 2017, she is walking down the aisle. Yes! Emily is getting married.

Our beautiful Emily continues on her journey through life. She is undeniably unstoppable. She is an inspiration and a demonstration of what is possible when you keep moving forward.

(March 2017 – 2 weeks before Emily's wedding.)

ABOUT LINDA MALLARD

 Linda started teaching movement at the age of 12. As a gymnast and then coach, Linda loved teaching and helping others succeed. She later attended the University of British Columbia in Physical Education and began teaching adults in the world of fitness and health.

After years of working in fitness clubs as a personal trainer, corporate health manager and instructor trainer, Linda wanted to get back to a one on one and small group focus. Her passion is about making a difference with each and every client.

Since 2001, Linda has owned the Tsawwassen Wellness Centre, a boutique Pilates and Mindful Movement Studio. She loves teaching full time, but also being immersed in her community. Linda's focus is on creating opportunity for her clients to LIVE BY CHOICE. That they have the health and strength to do whatever matters to them in their life.

While Pilates benefits all body's, Linda's passion is in rehabilitation and with the aging population. To see client's having fun, living with purpose and continuing to explore and expand is what has her put her feet on the floor each day.

At 50 something, Linda loves to trail run, ski and play. She is the mother of 3 amazing children and lives and works in her community.

JESS' STORY...

by Chuck and Roxanne Marbes

I was a young single Mom when my son, Brady, had his first seizure in December 1999 at 3 months old. That is the day I started stress eating. For every seizure (he had 5-10 daily and tens of thousands throughout his life), hospitalization, surgery or other painful procedure Brady endured, I began to eat more and use food as therapy. I realized I was gaining weight, not exercising and was generally unhealthy and not taking care of myself, but couldn't see a way of changing as I worked full-time and devoted every other minute to my children. We had everything because we had each other. Our life wasn't easy by any means (his disease didn't take breaks for vacations or holidays), but we lived EVERY day to the fullest! We had more adventures in Brady's 13 1/2 years than most will in a lifetime.

On the morning of May 30, 2013, I walked across the house to get Brady up for school and noticed an eerie quietness. As usual that morning, I said, "Hey Buddy, time to get up," and he usually greeted me with a sweet coo in response. But that day was different. He didn't respond, and I saw no movement when I got in his room. He was clearly not breathing. I began screaming and rubbing his arm telling him to breathe. My daughter ran to his room with my phone and we called 911. I administered CPR until the paramedics arrived and they brought him to our family room, put an AED on his chest, and he was pronounced dead shortly after. In fact, one of my childhood friends was the one who told me Brady was gone. My baby boy, my right-hand man who was at my side for all his sister's sporting events, every shopping trip, vacation, holiday, birthday, the boy who endured over 20 surgeries and 35 hospitalizations and countless other painful procedures, was gone. He had been thru so much and passed away in his sleep, without me there to hold his hand like I did for every other thing in his life. My life revolved around taking care of Brady and being my daughter, McKenzie's, biggest fan and support system. I was looking forward to McKenzie going to college and being a kid herself as she had to grow-up too fast seeing all her brother went thru. I had plans for Brady and me. We were going to be the next Team Voyt, doing marathons and triathlons and visiting McKenzie at college, and spoiling her when we could.

I used Brady's medical conditions and death as excuse to eat unhealthy and not exercise. I put my heart and soul into being the best Mom I could be for my two beautiful children and, for me. That meant not taking any time for myself because I was not willing to spend a minute apart from them, besides when I worked each day. I developed these unhealthy habits over 16 years and change is hard, especially when I was using food as a way to relieve stress. Grieving the loss of my son was a pain and heartache I never thought I would have to experience. I knew I could not continue these habits and avoid major health issues, so I joined a gym and started doing several hours of cardio each night. I did lose some weight.

In January 2016, right after my daughter, McKenzie, went back to school after Christmas break, I was in a MAJOR funk. My future had always included taking care of and enjoying time with Brady (forever), and without him and Kenz back at school. I had an empty house. It was something I had never experienced and never thought I would. I was incredibly lost! I was a Mom at 21 years old, and that is all I knew and all I wanted or needed. My life was complete, and in the blink of an eye, that all changed. Brady was gone and two years later Kenz was off to college. As they say, the Lord works in mysterious ways and I was so lucky. He pointed me to a Facebook advertisement for a Better Body Fitness 28 Day Challenge. I was even luckier my friend, Kathy Jacobs, agreed to join me. It is always easier walking in the door to the unknown with a friend and having an accountability partner.

The morning of orientation, the coaches explained the High/Low Diet and put us thru a workout with the other newbies. I remember being in awe of the athletes and members I saw working out at BBF. It was hard to imagine I could ever get in shape or keep up with these people, but I wanted that in the worst way. I was always an athlete, and I immediately felt that competitive side coming back and a hunger to get healthy and lose weight. I saw the coaches pushing the seasoned members and, after my second official workout, I told one of the coaches that he could push me as much as he sees fit, especially if he sees me not putting in the effort. He told me that he usually gives new members three days before he unleashes his "encouragement." By the fourth day, I started hearing my name more, and the coaches were pushing me to do things I did not think I could do. I definitely would have never pushed myself to do them.

I was so out of shape that at orientation, I thought the warm-up was the actual workout. Little did I know we still had a workout, finisher and stretching to get through. I didn't know how I would get thru one week, much less 28 days, and not only did I do that, but I joined after the 28 Day Challenge. I continued to lose almost 60 pounds total in the year since I have been a member. Before joining BBF, I was eating what I wanted whenever I wanted. Better Body Fitness introduced me to the

High-Low Meal Plan and it was actually fairly easy to follow compared to other plans I have tried. It takes planning and meal prepping but I don't feel like I am depriving myself and I feel like I am set up for success in a plan that works for me. The plan came with a recommended list of foods to stick to. I also felt like if I had a piece of cake or bad meal, it was ok, as long as it wasn't a daily habit. At the beginning my muscles were sore after each work out (for days), and there were days I didn't want to go. I actually almost drove past the building once but knew my friends would be wondering where I was. I couldn't lie and would feel too guilty to say I just didn't want to go. I eventually became addicted to Bootcamp and looked forward to seeing these new friends every day. The Bootcamps are all planned out for us and work every part of our bodies. We are taught how to do the exercises correctly, resulting in weight loss, muscle gain, and injury prevention. We are in and out in under an hour during the week and just over an hour on Saturday. It is the right combination of coaches, "diet," workout and the exact right time for me. I believe that is why I have been successful.

I started seeing results on the scale and my friends, family and co-workers were noticing, too. I was improving skills on the gym floor and doing things, like box jumps, that terrified me in the beginning. Then I started to look forward to doing them to see how much I improved from week to week. I started believing in myself because the coaches believed in me. I hate to admit it, but I actually started to enjoy burpees! I'm not a person who likes attention or to receive compliments, but when people started noticing my weight loss, it made me want to work harder because people were proud of the hard work I was putting in and actually asking me for advice. There were people who did not recognize me because of the physical changes. People also started noticing not only the weight loss, but the toning. I actually had visible muscles. Of course, when a woman is as overweight as I was, we want results overnight and when going from very limited physical activity to six days a week, we do one burpee and expect to be a size 4. It didn't exactly happen like that, but I was losing weight each month and making improvements on the gym floor.

Four months after my journey started at BBF, my daughter and I completed our first Spartan race with some of the coaches and friends we met at BBF. It was over 100 degrees with the heat index and over 5 miles and 23 obstacles. I never dreamed I would be doing an obstacle course race, much less completing one and wanting to do more.

Before I joined BBF, my back and feet hurt all the time, and I thought it was from all of the years of lifting my son out of his wheelchair. In reality, it was from the extra weight and lack of physical activity. I was not getting the results as quickly as I wanted at the other gym. I didn't have support of coaches there and didn't know what I needed to do to get results.

In one short year at BBF, I went from a lost soul who was completely out of shape, in pain and overweight, to losing almost 60 lbs., gaining countless new friends who inspire me daily and having a healthy outlet to deal with my grief. I, physically, feel better than I can remember. I never want to go back to where I was and honestly I can't afford it for my health or my wallet.

It's true. You have to be in the right mind set, you have to want it. If you have that and the support like I do from the coaches and people at BBF, anything is possible. You will reach your goals! BBF sets their members up for success by giving us a plan in and out of the gym.

There are so many things that keep me coming back to BBF; the owners and coaches who have put a successful plan together with proven results, the members who are now friends who I look forward to seeing every day, the results I have seen and the fear of gaining weight back and becoming unhealthy (my Mom has Type 2 Diabetes, has had a heart attack and my Dad has high blood pressure). I also love the fire that BBF has reignited in me and my daughter which seemed impossible after such a big loss. Bootcamp is now a habit for me and built in to every day of the week, and there is something missing if I cannot make it even one day. I have tried other weight loss/diet plans dozens of times, and was a member at other gyms where I would work out for twice as long and not see results. I now have a place to go every night after work and friends who I look forward to seeing.

I was embarrassed of my size and afraid to walk in the gym and have fit, healthy people judge me because I was so out of shape. The day I walked in the door at BBF, the people were not judgmental at all. Actually, they were just the opposite. Everyone is focused on getting and staying healthy and encouraging people around them when working out. The coaches are there to help you become successful, make sure you do the moves properly and do not injure yourself. They plan out every work out and work every part of your body so all you have to do is show up. I am not one to talk about my feelings or go to a therapist, so Bootcamp became my therapy and eating healthy became our lifestyle. If I was having a bad day, missing and grieving Brady, I would go to Bootcamp and work even harder to get those frustrations and feelings out. Before BBF, I would just go eat a cookie the size of my head. I, *finally*, have a healthy outlet. We all have to start somewhere, and I am so glad I stumbled upon BBF. It has changed our life, and I don't ever want to go back to where I was a year ago. I can't wait to see what the future has to hold! It does not matter what level of fitness you are, BBF modifies each workout for all abilities, and I promise you will not regret taking that first step.

Pictures of Jess and Jess with her Daughter Kenzie

ABOUT CHUCK AND
ROXANNE MARBES

My name is Chuck Marbes and, along with my beautiful wife, Roxanne, we own and operate Better Body Fitness in Green Bay, WI. We are a body transformation center that specializes in helping our clients lose fat, build muscle, and, most importantly, have fun. Roxanne and I have over 15 years of combined professional experience inside the fitness industry and have worked with over a thousand clients.

At BBF we believe community, support, and accountability are three of the biggest keys to a client's success. We also believe that environment, both physically and socially, can and will shape a client's outcome. So, at BBF we set out on a mission to create a safe, welcoming, supportive and highly educational environment.

We like to think of BBF as the Cheers of the fitness industry – a place where everybody knows your name. It is a place where you can't wait to go to whether it's the crack of dawn or after a long, hard day of work. We want to be the brightest spot in our client's day. We believe as much in helping our clients create amazing body transformations

SCRIPTOR PUBLISHING GROUP

as we do building relationships. You must enjoy the process. At BBF, building stronger and more fit bodies is just as important as building new friendships.

Getting our clients results is our number one focus and we do that with an incredible team of coaches and an incredible community of members. We work together to help each other achieve greatness and life changing transformations. We are the Better Body Fitness Family.

158

TRANSFORMATION

by Mike Marcinek

Transformation.

It is such a buzz word in the Fitness Industry. It seems as if every other ad promises that you can lose 20lbs in 6 weeks or "x" number of inches so you can fit into that bathing suit.

I do not think you can undersell the power of transformation any more than by reducing it to mere pounds and inches. If we are to truly transform ourselves, I don't believe that means to simply become a smaller version of what we are now or to wear the next size down. Now, it may often begin that way but rarely does it end there. I believe that transformation means to evolve into something more. Transformation can change your health, your outlook, your appreciation, your perspective and yes, your life!

I know this. I see it happen every day. I am able to walk in to my facility, NEPA Fit Club, on a daily basis and see people making massive dramatic changes to their physical, mental emotional selves.

The funny thing is, this is never where I intended to be. So how did I get here? Well, transformation of course. Like so many other transformations however, the road is rarely linear. It involves sharp emotional turns and difficult conversations about where you think your happiness may lie and where it actually is.

My story actually starts at the high school pool. Now, if you had a pool in your high school it may not be that difficult to be brought back to the thick humid air hanging over you while the distinct smell of chlorine burns your nostrils. Having just come to my local public high school from a life of small Catholic elementary schools, I may as well have been walking the streets of a foreign city. I barely knew any of the names or faces of the people who surrounded me. While everyone around me was, seemingly, ecstatic to break up the monotony of Algebra and World History, all I could think of is that air and that smell. Every step into that room intensified the air and that chemical aroma that elicited a Pavlovian response of fear. See, I knew as the air got heavier and the smell got stronger, that we were one step closer to having to get into that water. That meant one step closer to having to take my shirt off, or in this case, not take it off.

I don't know if you could think all the way back to being 14 or 15 years old, but the opposite sex, they were kind of a big thing. Who am I kidding? They were, kind of, everything, and at 5'7, 240lbs -falling firmly into the bracket of childhood obesity - I would not easily catch their eye. In fact, when you find yourself at that size, at that age, you try to do as much as you can to NOT bring attention to yourself. Unfortunately, keeping your shirt on in the pool does not fall under that category. I remember keeping my eyes firmly affixed at my feet as I walked across the damp tile floor, hoping to sneak by, unnoticed. Meanwhile, hormone soaked classmates with six packs performed cannonballs and flips trying to prove themselves to be at the top of the adolescent animal kingdom. Meekly stepping your chubby toes into the water with an XXL t-shirt about to cling to your body, sort of tips the attention scale in the opposite direction.

At that moment, I decided I was going to transform myself, not just lose weight. My parents cared about my well-being. They took me to see dietitians, and I had lost weight and gained weight. Rinse and repeat -over and over. Now, it was time for massive change.

I read, voraciously, on nutrition and working out. I joined the football team. I would work out, go to practice come home and work out. My food was measured and weighed. My mother was admonished for anything less than 90% lean beef or any additional butter and oil. I began taking supplements. When I went out for the football team at 5'7, 240lbs, I was an overweight slow nose guard. As a senior I was an undersized, quick 5'7 167lb nose guard that was pretty much solid muscle. I bench pressed 300lbs. I squatted well over 500 and did chin ups with 100lbs hanging off my body. I had transformed myself. But was it for the better?

Not all transformations are for the best. I had gotten leaner, I had gotten stronger. Those were my goals, and I had reached them, but at what cost? I had become obsessed with the gym. I didn't follow sports that I loved as closely because I was too busy working out or reading about working out. I avoided parties. I fought with my family, constantly, about dinner choices and the food that was made. In the greatest irony of all, even though it was my embarrassment around the opposite sex that pushed me to take on this massive change, I was now avoiding dates with the girls I had hoped to catch so much as a fleeting glance from, just because they may involve pizza or ice cream.

My transformation had led me to obsession. Fortunately, I used this obsession with nutrition as platform to pursue a degree in Nutrition and Dietetics and become a registered Dietitian. It was on this path that I learned that what was once such a positive - transforming my physical appearance- never really left me with the confidence I needed. What it had left me with was a rigid diet that included eating the same exact breakfast for over 3 years. I was also obsessively exercising any time a sweet or snack would hit my lips and distancing myself from others to avoid situations that involved food. My education led me to discover that I, in fact, had a type of bulimia nervosa.

This discovery led me to bring order back into my life. I started to develop positive relationships with food again. I started to meet people out over dinner or coffee. My added calorie intake helped fuel my workouts and to realize that I wasn't going to go back to that obese little kid overnight. Everything was going great - until I hurt my back.

Invincibility, it seems, mostly only works in the comics. Try telling that to someone in their early 20's. I remember the day like it was yesterday. I can remember the sound of clanking weights and heavy metal music, and I can feel my dry chalked up hands and see a mostly empty gym, all to myself ("meathead paradise"). I had just finished a heavy squat/bench workout and was going finish up with some rows on the cable machine when I felt a little twinge in my low back. This was new for me, so I stopped, got up and, like any good meathead would do, I tried again. No good, it was there again, but this time it was worse. I remember walking out of the gym and each step to my car getting progressively worse. I then remember barely being able to stand up when trying to get out of the car and into my house.

The next few months were hell. It would take me hours until I could walk with the pain reduced enough to get through my day. I would often need help putting my socks on in the morning. Think about that. I went from being a guy who would receive medals for picking hundreds of pounds off the floor, to a guy who needed his mom to help him put on his socks.

It was humbling to say the least.

I was given two options from my doctor. The first was immediate surgery. When I told him that I'd like to avoid back surgery in my early 20's, he responded with, "Ok, then ice and Advil" Gee, thanks doc! Quite the wide spectrum for treatment there. So, after numerous attempts at trying to push through the pain, I decided I had to transform the way that I looked at my training. It was not just about numbers. Training had to "give back" and not just take away. I, once again, took to reading voraciously, ran up credit card debt while seeking out experts and information and emerged from this episode with a different understanding.

This experience led me to want to help others. I wanted to help others avoid debilitating injury. I wanted others to avoid obsessive, restrictive eating plans that could crush their performance. I was determined that I would open my own facility and help others achieve their goals!

It is just that, while I had transformed my thoughts on how to go about training, I was not completely prepared to "shake off all of the meathead." When I opened my facility, I envisioned myself training athletes, powerlifters, Olympic lifters, and the like, to get really big, really strong and to crush these awesome workouts. We would discuss fancy lifting techniques and technical programs. We would go over peaking and cycling and nutrient timing. I would help them avoid injury. They were going to dominate and this was going to be awesome.

Well, a funny thing happened on the way to the forum.

Clients did show up - a good bunch of them, in fact. And 95% of them were 37-55 year-old women.

Suddenly my grand design of that old school dank gym where success was tracked purely in pounds on the bar or reps in your journal was no longer on the table. Something even more incredible happened, though. This clientele who initially came to me to have me help their jeans fit a

163

little looser, allowed me to unlock and realize the transformation that had been occurring within myself. Every single one of my experiences had led me to this point. I too, had struggled with nutrition. I had struggled with injury. Each one of those experiences had allowed me to change the definition of myself. I no longer identified with a body fat percentage, or a waist size. It wasn't about the numbers on the bar or in the journal. It was about perspective and growth.

Seeing these women come to me, and hearing their stories, allowed me to understand that while their goal may be to lose weight, their "why" was way more than a number on a scale. Their 'why' was their families. It was their experiences and their friends. Once we were able to offer perspective, we were able to open the door for growth. Once this perspective infected our facility, the growth of our clients led to a rapid change in culture. This culture is evident every day and is one that I am proud and humbled to get to witness.

It is seen in the over 2 dozen women who set their alarms for 4:30 in the morning and are barely awake as they hear the first splashes of coffee rattle their mug. While many others are sound asleep, they are getting ready to train at our 5:30am group class. Within sixty minutes they are swinging kettlebells and high fiving each other. The easy decision would be to hit snooze and catch up on another 15-min rest. The change in their mindset allows them to realize that they are transforming their habits and investing in themselves.

It can be seen in Christina who was so timid at first that she had to have some else make her initial appointment (and struggled to make eye contact). Her first session she did 0 pushups - as in none. As each session went on, we could see more progress. She walked taller, and 20 pushups later, she passed her test to work for the state of Pennsylvania and transformed her fear into strength, confidence and a career.

Virginia came to us at 80 years young. When so many others would be hesitant to leave the house, let alone walk in to a gym filled with kettlebells, ropes and barbells, she chose to stay. In the meantime, she shed the idea that she was defined by her age and her past. At 81 years of age, she deadlifted 135lbs and a DEXA scan revealed a 10% increase in her bone density!

Anita came to us after a time of loss in her life, frustrated, upset and emotional as anyone would be. She struggled for goals and for definition. In the process, she found how strong she could be and set an example for her daughters. Now she is passing that strength, consistency, and persistence down to them and everyone they encounter.

There is also Jean Marie, who, having tried every cardio program there was, came to us with a goal of weight loss and found herself a powerlifting medalist along the way. She eventually did reach those weight loss goals, in time for her daughter's wedding. Those photos will serve as a lifetime reminder that through strength confidence and consistency, anything can be achieved.

Through my own experiences, I recognize that not every transformation is linear. There are struggles. There are victories where you climb to the top, only to lose your footing and slip a bit. Every journey, however, is buoyed by your "why." Your "why" gives you perspective and purpose.

The evolution I experienced in my life has given me the opportunity to witness this culture of transformation at our facility. While we still do train athletes and men, I'm not sure I could truly have the perspective that I carry with me this day if I did not get to the chance to transform what I valued in fitness. I quickly realized that fitness itself was not where the value lied at all. Fitness was just a catalyst to unlock the inner strength and perspective that truly changes lives.

Do not hold yourself hostage to numbers, whether they be on the scale or sewn to the inside of your waistband. There is so much more to you, so much more that defines you, and so much that you are left to become. Once you realize this and embrace the opportunity, you will transform yourself in a way that no advertisement could ever define.

About Mike Marcinek

After all the letters and credentials, Mike Marcinek simply wants to be known as someone who cares. Struggling with obesity during adolescence, he had endured the struggles of being overweight during an awkward time and also dealing with those who said they cared to help, but did not follow through on their words.

Determined to overcome his obstacles, Mike turned to sports to help get him active. This lead to a love of fitness and exercise as well as countless hours spent reading and studying nutrition. Mike would go on to earn a bachelor's degree in Nutrition and Dietetics as well as a Master's degree in Sports Nutrition and Exercise Science.

Mike's own transformation and passion for fitness and nutrition, led him to start NEPA Fit Club and Driven Athletics in Blakely, PA, where he has trained everyone from state record holders and professional athletes to grandmothers alongside their grandchild.

Mike resides in Northeast PA with his wife, Danielle and their two dogs, Oliver and Alfie.

A Story of a Real Life Super Momma

by Tera Mathis

It was 5 years ago at a health fair that I met Loretta. I love helping busy overwhelmed mommas reclaim their birthright to be better. To be stronger mentally, emotionally and physically. It is my passion.

Loretta stopped by my booth briefly to chat. I could tell she was curious but definitely not super excited about the idea of change or commitment. She seemed at peace with her level of health and fitness at that point. Loretta moved on that day. I did not hear from her again until the fall of 2016.

In August of 2016 Loretta reached out to me via Facebook. I invited her into the studio for a visit. When she walked through the doors I was met with a completely different Loretta. I saw a beat down, overwhelmed, exhausted and frustrated woman. She was being crushed by the responsibilities of her life. I soon found out that she is a mother, wife and excellent nurse. Loretta does an EPIC job of taking care of others, but at an extremely high cost to her own well-being.

Loretta was your modern day Super Momma. She would bend over backwards for her family, friends, church and job but could not allow herself the time to take care of Loretta. And on the rare occasions she would go on outings with her family Loretta would end up physically paying for it days afterward because of the poor health her body was in.

The stress of life and the lack of making time for herself showed in her eyes. By ignoring her own health and fitness she found herself with fatty liver disease, constant pain, blood pressure issues and she was pre-diabetic. She was physically and mentally exhausted the day she walked into my studio.

We had an amazing chat that day. There may even have been some tears from both of us.

What were some of the inner thoughts and beliefs she carried that kept her from being healthy, strong and taking care of herself, you ask? Let me share a few:

- I am a selfish momma and wife if I take 1 hour 3 x week to train my body and mind.

- I am a selfish momma if I make the financial investment to work with a trainer 3 x week.

- I am to busy at work and home to come train 3 x week

- I should be spending more time with my family.

- My husband cooks and I'm not worthy of asking him to cook a special diet.

- It is so expensive to eat healthy food.

- I have tried 3 different gyms and a dietician and they didn't help me.

- I typically don't stick to an exercise routine for more than a month or two at a time.

- I always give up because I don't see results."

Sound familiar? These thoughts and behaviors are VERY similar to many of the mommas I work with.

These were some of Loretta's "stories". To Loretta they were absolutely true. She wasn't sure they could ever be changed. These stories had made her last 3 years very challenging in a not so serving way and her health was showing the effects.

That hot August day she stood at the proverbial fork in the road. She had a choice to make. She could choose the path on the left. Make the same daily choices she had year after year and get weaker, fatter and sicker. Taking this fork would not only affect her own health but also the wellbeing of her family and patients. She would not be able to participate and thrive in life. Someone would be taking care of her.

OR>>>>

She could choose the path to the right. A new and unexplored path. A scary and unknown path. One that would challenge her beliefs and push her out of her comfort zone daily. A path where I could teach her to thrive. And not just in the gym. But thrive in life. To live a BIG and FULL life. One that would help her reclaim her birthright to be better. To be Stronger. To be Healthier. To be Happier. To be More confident. To Better to serve others.

How teachable and coachable was she going to be? Was she going to be open minded and experiment with new and different foods? Was she going to be open minded toward the mindset journaling and tools? Was she going to be open minded and try new and different movements? Was she going to be adaptable?

Or was she going to walk away and continue down the tried and true path? The "safe" and know path?

170

Loretta chose the path on the right. She stepped up and chose to pursue a BIG life. She took personal responsibility for her wellbeing and health.

She started coming into the studio consistently 3 time per week for 45 minutes. Was it easy? NO. Absolutely not. It was her commitment to herself, her personal responsibility and drive that kept her coming in week after week. We modified. We adapted. We focused on what she could do and where she could move. We began to build a stronger, more confident and healthier Loretta.

She started working through her subconscious stories that were holding her back and keeping her in the same unhealthy cycle of self-neglect. This was a scary and challenging process for Loretta. She developed a powerful, growth centric mindset that will serve her forever using the tools and systems I shared with her.

I taught her to use a dictate journal to uncover and bring awareness to what her subconscious drivers and stories were. We also implemented mantras and used an awareness dot. These tools help Loretta take personal responsibility for those stories and is helping her change them.

She took control of her nutrition and food choices. She learned about building healthy sustainable habits at a subconscious level. These habits have helped Loretta create a healthier, stronger and leaner version of herself. She learned about different macronutrients and how they work for her body.

This was all a journey and took time and consistent daily intentional effort. Team Loretta and Tera worked together consistently for 6 months. Layering in changes piece by piece. Backing up when we needed to and pushing forward when she was ready. She has been completely teachable and coachable to the process and tools I have shared with her and she has been successful in transforming into a strong and healthy Momma.

From Loretta, "Initially I started working with Tera to help me lose some weight. I have gained so much more from her coaching on mindset, nutrition and exercise. Prior to working out with Tera I was scared to exercise because of problems with my neck and herniated disk. She individualized my workout and now I'm stronger than I have been for years with less pain."

Loretta no longer has fatty liver disease. She no longer struggles with blood pressure or blood sugar issues. She went from 34% body fat to 20% body fat, shedding over 5 inches in her belly alone. Loretta has completely changed the shape of her body. There is a light in her eyes and she is not hunched over from the stresses of life. She is excited to conquer the challenges life throws at her in any situation.

The physical transformation has been something to see but the mindset shift in Loretta has been the most impactful transformation for me to witness. She takes time for herself and knows how important taking care of Loretta first is. She loves herself and is excited to take care of her mind, body and soul. She has stepped into her power and I absolutely cannot wait to see everything she accomplishes going forward.

ABOUT TERA MATHIS

Tera Mathis is a speaker and coach. She trains youth as well as busy Mommas to become healthy and strong. She teaches them to reclaim their birthright to be better. To be healthy. To be strong. Tera has two studios she where she trains small groups and private sessions. She does distance training as well.

Tera is passionate about helping others become and create the best version of themselves. Teaching them to be healthy and confident and live an inspired life. Her 365 Strong program for both youth and Mommas focuses on mindset, nutrition and movement. This trifecta has been the most effective at helping people create life-long health and wellness.

Website: Www.teramathis.com

Email: 365strongmommas@gmail.com

Facebook: https://m.facebook.com/KettlebellSynergies/

180 DEGREES

by Jodi Molitor

I grew up a small-town girl in northern Minnesota. I guess you could say I was an average size kid, not really having any weight issues. What I did know was that I did not want the heartache of some of my close friends and family who struggled with weight and confidence issues. I love my family and needed to find a way of living that would keep my predisposed genetics from being my crutch. Being on the high school swim team left nothing to hide.

I learned early on how to swallow my pride and get over how my body looked. I just accepted it...kind of.

I left the nest to college and was on my own. Out of safety of my parents' home, it was all me trying to figure out a healthy plan to get fit and stay motivated. Being that I like people, I gathered all those I could to start working out with me. Whether it was sweating out our previous night college beer binges or poor eating habits at the local gym, I suckered them into joining me. I even made them endure innumerable rollerblading excursions!

We always had fun though. I learned early on that if I didn't plan the outings, they did not happen. That piece of knowledge would prove to be useful in later phases of my life.

Now working a full-time job and living on my own, the pressures of REAL life were in my face. I still liked to be active and gathered whoever wanted to hang with me, mostly my poor high school sweetheart husband. My eating habits got worse, and I rapidly gained weight (45 lbs. to be exact) and started to lose sight of being physically active. Relying on the "eating very little" diet and grabbing whatever unhealthy snack I could grab caused my metabolism to slow down to a near stop. I was losing the muscle I had at a rapid pace. Fitness became less important and I lost energy and drive to want to exercise. This was not a happy or attractive stage for me.

Depressed and fat due to lack of endorphins and blood flow which I had become accustomed to from being physically active, I knew I needed to get back to my natural "happy pill". So I took hold of my situation and started the latest trend at that time - steady state cardio and a low fat diet plan. Did I lose weight? You bet I did! I also lost muscle and did not fix my already-destroyed metabolism. I made it worse. Loving my new look and weight loss, I gathered others who wanted to do what I was doing. Looking back this makes me laugh! It was great having co- workers and friends who shared in the same passion as me, even if I was the driving force, and they thought I was nuts. Years later, while pregnant with our first child, Jacob (now 18), my low fat, cardio only, lifestyle blew up in my face.

I was a very crabby pregnant person. I was very ill, not bedridden, but morning, noon and night sickness the ENTIRE 9 months. I was also a pro at gaining weight, I was trying to pretend to be happy as I was quickly watching all my years of hard work balloon up. When I say quickly, I mean 40 pounds by 20 weeks and with a total of 75 pounds by my son's birth! NOT cute! I tried to laugh it off, but it was occupying all my heart and soul and hurting relationships.

Even the nurses thought I had gestational diabetes since I had ballooned up all on my own. Nope, sorry just getting fat no medical diagnosis for that! I was the product of my messed-up metabolism from a low-fat diet and no muscle from a cardio-only fitness routine.

The struggle was real, and I was determined to fight back. I strapped my boy on my chest or back and hit the trails and frozen Minnesota lakes as soon as I was able to walk again. A now- determined to lose the weight and stay-at-home Mom, I took whatever chance I had, to keep moving and use proper nutrition and portion control. Then came another road block - baby #2!

It was one baby after another (3 under 4 years to be exact), several job changes for Hubby, and a few housing moves to know that we were officially in the throes of life. I focused all my attention on my little growing family and did not make time for myself. I remained insecure about my now-changed body, and I had no time to fix it! Not satisfied with my current look and the way I physically, mentally and spiritually felt, I sought out different exercise routines and ways to fill the void.

Then it happened….

I was doing whatever I could to get in shape, finally making time for fitness now that the kids were a little older and two of the three in school. Little did I know that on a weekend at my parents' lake home, it all would come crashing down on me.

This was the start of an awesome, crazy, unpredictable journey.

It was a hot July day on beautiful Lake Vermilion, and I was trying to wakeboard for the first time. I was supposed to hold on and let the boat pull me up to pop into position. Well, it didn't quite happen that way. I popped something, but not up on top the wake behind the boat. Instead,

I felt a crack in my back which was instantly painful, and I knew right there that this was not going to be good.

For about 6 months I struggled with pain, depression and weight gain. Through rehab, MRI's, acupuncture, chiropractic care, physical therapy, plenty of pain killers and muscle relaxers to kill a horse, I did not get the answers needed to get well. I could not even sleep, sit upright or bend over without pain. All of the testing was done without ever really having a diagnosis to my pain caused by the accident. I was not in a good place physically or mentally.

Seeking out comfort and a way to strengthen my back, I had tried several strength training programs to no avail. I one day stumbled upon a nutrition shop in the next small town over. I thought maybe I could find a quick fix of a fat burning pill or whatever they might recommend to get me well.

What's that thing?

Yeah, I want to try that!

A kettlebell and a few other functional tools were part of this tiny personal training space in back of the nutrition shop. I had never seen a kettlebell before and was very intrigued to see if this might be my miracle fix.

I started right then and there in my jeans because I knew that if I went home I wouldn't go back. Two weeks later, my back pain disappeared, and I was on my way to strengthening my core. I actually felt better and was hopeful for the first time since attempting wakeboarding.

Shortly after starting this program I went home to chat with my stay-at-home buddy about these bells that I loved. He thought I was crazy and loved it all at the same time. I literally bought one 12 kg kettlebell with my birthday money and brought just that one over to his house for both of us to use. He had no option but to workout with me! Our bodies transformed, and we started a craze in the neighborhood. I asked him "what do you think about me starting a gym doing this?"

He laughed hysterically with me and said, "Good luck!"

I had the drive and a vision to reach our community with my passion for fitness. With that 180 Kettlebell Gym was born. My eyes have been opened to the reality of how deep this vision has touched many. We have been able to be part of people's most intimate depths of their soul and share in countless triumphs and sorrows. For me this is what it's all about. Their stories all hold special place in my heart. I am honored to have been given this beautiful gift of touching lives and they have gifted mine just as much or more. What a blessing it has been.

Our story has been extremely difficult, challenging and heart breaking. This business is not for the thin blooded person. We have had many wins and many failures along the way. Some have been very hurtful and painful which have left scars, but they all have shaped and molded me to be better at what I do and closer to those I love. Our family and friends have grown and endured right alongside us. There is no way we would be here today without them supporting us every ugly and beautiful step of the way. They truly get "doing life" and walking through the fire right with us. All the good and bad have made us the leaders in our industry for people seeking life changing body transforming lives.

Hence the name of the gym - 180.

We exist to be the change factor that people use to turn their lives from where they are to where they were meant to go. Making a 180 change happens one degree at a time.

The rewards of getting to share others' achievements and goals, whatever they might be, is worth every tear and sleepless night for that moment

178

of pure joy and gratitude. We are truly blessed to have been surrounded by, and worked with, so many amazing people.

—" I have turned 180 degrees myself after the accident. I took my body and mind from where I was to where I want to be. I'm not there yet but I will continue to strive for excellence not perfection. It brings me great joy to be able to help others achieve their 180 degree change one degree at a time.

About Jodi Molitor

Jodi Molitor is a leading expert in the field of transforming thousands of men, women and young athletes to reach their fitness and personal life goals. She is an organic entrepreneur that has always had a passion for helping others achieve their goals and building them up to their full potential. The struggle is real with no celebrity endorsements or financial gifts of any sort, her and her husband have built their fitness facilities up to near full capacity with each program being sold out as they launch. Her and her team are passionate and take seriously how the tools they use to shape and mold people are a gift. Perseverance and No Regrets is the mantra of 180 Kettlebell Gym. And living to hear the words "well done" is the goal of every decision.

FROM FEAR TO EXCITEMENT

By Daythan Nottke

For me, fitness has always been a coping tool - a form of therapy. As a youth, I struggled with severe drug addiction which eventually led me to drop out of high school and begin participating in criminal activities. By the time I was 21, I had been to prison two times. It was here that I discovered the gift of the human body and began to study and practice the art of fitness. It was my escape, my passion, and very quickly became my way of life.

When I was released in 2013, my prospects for gainful employment and assimilating into regular society were grim. However, my passion for fitness endured. In fact, I would go as far as to say that the reason I had such a hard time finding a job was because I was so focused on my training inside, and my nutrition outside of the gym.

I met my wife at this time, and she became pregnant with my first son. This was a blessing and a curse as I had no real job, and we were living with my parents at the time. So, this is where I committed to becoming a Personal Trainer so that I could use my gifts and live my passion, while providing a stable lifestyle for my family. While working fast food during the day, mopping the floors at my gym during the midnight hours, and studying for my CPT whenever I could, I got certified and became a trainer.

181

Fast forward 3 years, and I am now the owner of two Women's Training Centers with over 300 members between both locations. All of my coaches (Including the one whose story I will share below) were my CLIENTS FIRST. They followed this program, got amazing results, got certified and are now spreading this awesome program to the lives of hundreds of women in our Community.

One thing that I have learned since entering the "business of fitness" three years ago is that this business has a funny way of bringing some amazing people into my life. It is natural, I suppose, since ours is a business of service.

One of these amazing clients is my friend, Mary. Mary is currently one of my top trainers, the General Manager of one of our Women's Training Facilities, an expert nutrition coach, as well as a close personal friend to me and my family. We are close enough to even share Thanksgiving dinner together.

When I met Mary, she had already lost a ton of weight. In fact, she had been studying to become a nutrition coach, and had already applied her knowledge to her own eating. She, like most women who see significant weight loss, felt stuck. She had tried running, cutting her calories back, and even tried the latest "Herbal Remedy" to get rid of unwanted bloat, and yet she still could not get past what she described as being "skinny fat". She had lost weight, but she wasn't toned.

Mary was standing at a gap. Where she stood on that first day was a scary place. Up until that point she had been killing herself during her runs (which were no longer getting results), and she was manically counting every calorie while starving her body of the nutrition she so desperately needed. She didn't want to be "bulky," and everyone has heard that lifting weights makes you look "big and buff!"

Where she stood on that first day was an extremely exciting place! She was at her wit's end, trying to figure out this "fitness" thing on her own. No matter how long or hard she ran, no matter how little she ate, she was STUCK! That is a feeling that goes deep. If we're not careful, we may start to believe that there is something wrong with us.

Being in the place that Mary was on her first day as my client is terrifying for many of the reasons I stated above. But mostly it is scary because it means that we are lost. We don't know how to take that next step towards our dreams......and this is when the excitement kicks in!

I was excited for Mary because I knew she was in a place where she would be willing to try all the things that she had been terrified to try before! That included less cardio and eating more food. Her excuses were, "But I'll get fat!" and "That's too many calories!" When we added in weight training, her excuse was, "I don't want to get bulky!"

When she found herself in a place that her commitment to her goals far outweighed her fear of the unknown, that is when her transformation could truly take place. I have been blessed enough to go through similar experiences with Coach Mary two other times over the course of our journey together.

The first was when we decided to open our own facility. We were working in the same box gym that I used to mop the floors in, and we were losing our business. The gym was going under, and we were feeling the pressure. So, I decided that, with the help of Mary and another one of our Clients-Turned-Coach, we would open a studio that would cater to the needs of Women over 30.

I was terrified! I was excited! And I found myself leaning on Coach Mary for the same support and guidance that I had been giving her not so long before.

The second time was when she made Body Burn her full time gig. That was hard for her. That was scary for me! It was scary to have someone depending on my business besides me! At the same time, we were so excited!

It meant our dream was real. It meant we were both 100% committed to seeing our little program turn into something powerful and amazing. Since then, neither one of us has ever looked back.

Mary's transformation from that first day to now has been such an integral part of the program that is changing so many lives in our community. From the nature of the workouts and our style of eating, to the structure of our accountability program, Coach Mary has been such a huge part of the forming of this program. It was originally designed for women like her.

There are a few key things here that I hope you get out of Mary's story, but if nothing else, you need to learn this: That moment when you are faced with the scariest challenge of your life - that moment when you are so terrified it is actually a little exciting. When you are facing the thing that has been keeping you up at night, the thing you have been thinking about every day for as long as you can remember....

That is your moment. That is YOUR THING! And it is ok that you are so scared you are about to pee your pants.....that is how you know it is right.

184

About Daythan Nottke

Coach Daythan NASM CPT is the Creator of Body Burn Women's Fitness Systems and the Owner of Body Burn Women's Fitness Franchise. He currently owns two Women's Training Centers and has more than 300 members between both locations.

Daythan's trainers were all clients first. They followed his training program, got amazing results, got certified and are now spreading this awesome program to the lives of hundreds of women in our Community.

One thing that he has learned since entering the "business of fitness" three years ago is that this business has a funny way of bringing some amazing people into his life.

For more information on their training programs, you can check out the Body Burn Women's Fitness Center at http://bodyburnwomensfitnesscenter.com.

KAIZEN

by Erik Peacock

I remember the day Tracy called, I almost blew it. We were doing a referral contest but apparently, I had shut my brain off. I usually am really good at prequalifying people, and especially someone referred by an active client. It should have been a slam dunk. During our conversation, at some point, I thought she just wanted to buy some nutrition products. Luckily as the conversation progressed I woke up and realized this was a person who was ready for a monumental change, and I rallied and got her in for a consultation.

Since then Tracy has been a model representation of what is possible. Her focus, determination endurance (especially this one), and humility has allowed her to be coached. It isn't easy to basically turn your health and fitness over to someone else.

The majority of our clients are women who are stuck. They are stuck in busy schedules they can't always control, and bodies that have betrayed them after having kids and the stress of being a parent. That same stress leads to subpar eating decisions and little or no exercise, until one day that moment comes – that, "WTF happened?" moment - when they see a picture of themselves or step on the scale and realize they are so far off track. There is a day where these women hit the "911 button" and decide enough is enough. That is when they do one or more of the following things:

A. Join a gym

B. Start a diet

C. Order some infomercial program

D. Hire a personal trainer

This day, luckily, Tracy chose "D."

I have watched her struggle, moving two steps forward then one step back, but never giving up. She always shows up with a great attitude on the outside despite struggling with her own self-image and guilt on the inside. Tracy is a role model for other women out there that it is possible to not only transform your body, but your life.

Will it be easy? No, despite what many scam artists say, selling false hope to separate you from your hard-earned money. It is your journey and, like any quest that is worth it, there will be obstacles, challenges and resistance along the way. Living an extraordinary life requires you to live an extra- ordinary life which means doing more than the average person does. Sadly, in our country right now, "ordinary" is overweight and sedentary. Tracy made the decision that was not for her- not with her physical health, not with her career and not with her life.

So, I am done talking. I can rant and rave about what a great, client, friend and person she is, but I will let her tell her story:

I was turning 40 and saw my physical health deteriorating. I was more confused than ever about what to do. I felt out of control and could not get my hormones into balance. I couldn't get the scale to move and when it did, it moved in the wrong direction. I finally decided that if I haven't figured it out by now, it was time to hire a professional.

Here I am four years later in the greatest shape of my life, and it didn't come easy. I am a slow learner, and it took a while for me to really figure out how important nutrition was. The saying "abs are made in the kitchen not the gym" is so true. I had been working out, but until I really gained the knowledge and clear understanding of what solid nutrition looked like, I didn't start seeing results. The great thing about Puravida Fitness is they let me keep coming back for review until it finally sank in. You simply can't get a big win with changing your body if you don't have your nutrition dialed in. This was a big milestone for me to finally get it.

Another thing I learned from my fitness journey is about life, about keeping the faith, how to create good habits and stay intentional. I learned to take my workout habits and parlay them into my business. I also learned that taking little actions everyday turns into tangible results. I use this experience in a lot of my professional speaking engagements to other women.

Probably one of the most defining moments in my journey was deciding to quit binge drinking on the weekends. I had been doing this for 10 years and it always left me beating myself up and not feeling accomplished. One of the things I strive for daily is to feel accomplished. It was hard to rally because not only physically did I feel crappy, but mentally as well. I finally recognized that if I was going to meet my physical goals and professional goals, I needed my best mindset. This habit was damaging my mindset each week, so it had to go.

I like things in black and white, and I do better with rules. I knew it had to be a drastic change. I had been journaling and reflecting on this idea. I realized this was a major obstacle in getting my mind where it needed to be. My mind is in a much better place now.

Mindset is first and foremost, and at Puravida Fitness, I was able to not just develop my muscles and body but I also developed my "discipline muscle." I now look and feel better at 44 than I have in years. I teach fitness and have a higher quality of life. My journey is not over, though. I look at this as lifelong that keeps evolving and moving forward.

Tracy's story to me because it shows how fitness is not just a 30 day quick fix or something you turn on and off it is a lifelong pursuit. I watched Tracy's physical transformation as she worked out here at Puravida Fitness but more importantly it was her transformation from within that really made the difference. No longer was this a knee jerk reaction turning 40 but a new lifestyle and way of thinking.

The great thing about Tracy is she stayed coachable and implemented everything we taught her. She is a model client to me not because she had great results but because she is a good representative of our core values and how important it is to have clients that fit your core values.

Our core values are Kaizen a Japanese word for constant steady improvement. She did this even though there were setbacks she kept moving forward and working on herself. Personal accountability is another one. Tracy took ownership of her situation we were the facilitators but she did the work. We can have the best programs but if a client puts it all on us they won't get results. She was accountable to herself and us and at the same time. She is a giver not a taker which is another core value of ours. She has a heart to help other women like herself and frequently encourages other clients who are struggling and or are new. She truly pays it forward. Finally, she has good life balance. The last thing we want someone to do is throw their family, their friends or their career under the bus by becoming obsessed with their workouts and eating where it is unhealthy. Tracy is a great mom, wife, and successful businesswoman. Despite being "busy" she finds a way to get it done and encourages others to do the same. Yes, she lost inches, body fat and weight but the real results are the person she became on the journey to do that.

ABOUT ERIK PEACOCK

Erik Peacock has always had a passion for health and wellness which started back as an athlete in high school and college. He earned his Bachelor of science degree from Minnesota State Mankato. Erik began his personal training career working for Northwest Athletic Clubs one of the biggest health club chains in the Minneapolis/St. Paul Area.

His passion and knowledge enabled him to become one of the top trainers in the Northwest Club system while managing a training staff. Although doing extremely well at Northwest, he envisioned a place where he could make a difference in people's lives outside of the constraints of the corporate world. In 2005, Erik left a lucrative personal training career to open up his own studio, Puravida Fitness which he has owned and operated since 2005.

Erik holds three accredited certifications and has helped hundreds of people achieve their fitness goals. He calls Puravida Fitness his ministry because he believes they not only transform bodies but lives as well. Giving back is as one of his core values and he is active supporting locals through sponsorship of events and activities to support those organizations. He currently resides in Apple Valley, Minnesota with his wife, Kymn, a stepson Brandon, and two daughters Alannah and Hailey.

RE-THINK, RE-AWAKEN AND RE-DEFINE

By Genesis Read

First off, I want to say I am extremely thankful to be a part of this project. I also appreciate anyone who takes the time to read, not only this story, but the many others in this book. You will definitely gain something out of your time investment.

Next, take a second to examine everything awesome about you. For real - take a second to do this. You can even write down the top 10 qualities about you. Pay attention to what comes to mind. Was it positive or negative? Did you say something like, "Well, damn, I'm a cool ass person. It will be hard to make that list." Or did you say something like, "I'm not good at anything"? If you did make a list or started to think about qualities you have, were there any that made you feel you do not deserve to be the best version of you?

The reason I ask you to do this is because you can have the best workout plans, best nutrition plans, and the best gym to attend, but if you are not mentally ready to believe in yourself with deep enough reasons to make a change, all that stuff will fade in the background. The most successful clients I have had have very deep, emotional reasons for making a change. They started with a little belief, and they took action. With a tiny bit of success, their belief kept growing.

Being a personal trainer I get the blessing of seeing people completely change who they are for the better. Through fitness, I have seen awesome new, romantic relationships develop, better jobs attained, health risk decreased, all types of confidence upgrades, and, most importantly, people who are able to operate at their best in life.

I was fortunate to be a part one inspirational fitness journey of our client, Lizeth Conseco. She is a mother of 2 and wife to an awesome supporter along her journey. Being encouraged by her significant other, Lizeth jumped in our program not knowing what to expect. One of the things I am grateful for is that she opened up about everything she wanted to change pretty early on. Some of the things she mentioned were depression, that her self-esteem was lower than ever, and she could not be active with her kids, let alone even go outside her house.

One moment I will never forget with Lizbeth was when she showed me a picture of her at one of her kids' birthday party. It was taken before she started on her health journey, and as she shared the story, she started crying. She said she could not believe who that person was and vowed never to go back. What hurt was the fact that, actually, she was embarrassed to take any pictures at her own kids' birthday party. That was a powerful moment for me and her. It reminded me how deep this fitness stuff gets.

Today this woman cannot stop talking pictures! It gives me such a good feeling to see Lizeth post pictures of herself in clothes she thought she could not wear. She also posts pictures of her cooking and prepping meals, and also of her and her man straight up enjoying their life. It's baffling to see the internal change.

I'm hoping some of this information is starting to reignite with your soul. It definitely takes work to make change but it is very possible.

What I want to do so is actually post some photos Lizbeth has sent to us over 10 months of being with us. Hopefully, this will encourage someone who is feeling similar in any type of way to get that spark to get them going. Below is a part of an email I received from Lizbeth. I wanted to share her exact words so you can relate in some type of way.

"Before joining GFT, I was unhappy very insecure, I didn't want to do anything fun with my family. I just wanted to be home. I was very depressed. I have struggled being overweight for years and never in a million years did I think I was able to take the steps I needed to take to better my health and self-esteem.

I didn't believe in myself at all. I hated the way I looked and felt all the time. Even when I signed up with GFT, I doubted myself. But thanks to my Boyfriend, Alicia and your support I got to where I am now. I slowly started to believe and feel confident about myself and being able to feel that is truly amazing... GFT gave me my life back and gave me the happiness that I had lost. I realized that I really wasn't living life before my fitness journey. Genesis, you are not just your typical trainer. You truly care about each and every one of your clients. You have become family but also a blessing to my life. I'm truly thankful for everything you have done for me.

I went from being 160 pounds to 115lbs. From being lazy and not ever wanting to go outside my home, to being active!! This allows me to have the energy to play with my kids. I never felt this happy and now living life on my terms. Now I love being be out. Fitness has become a passion of mine, I love it. I love working out, hiking, helping my kids stay active. Now there is a new me, living a new lifestyle."

Amazing, right? It gave me goose bumps as I copied it over to this page. One of the best things to come out of Lizbeth's transformation is the fact that she referred us over 5 people who have also completely changed their lifestyle as well. They, forever, have a different respect for her now. She had no idea she would impact so many people around her. She feels so strongly about her change, She continues to bring people into the GFT community, showing them what is possible. Our whole community is infected by her determination and hard work.

Again, hopefully, you can gain something out this story. Don't ever forget you deserve this!!! The power of fitness is real. Fitness and health does not require you to be special at all. It just requires you to commit to the process, and you can change your whole being. I believe you will, and if there is any chance you don't, simply reach out and we can help change that!

About Genesis Read

... ...|........... ....;;.. ...., ...

Hello my name is Genesis Read and I proudly own Genesis Fitness Training in San Marcos, Ca. That is little city about 20 mins north of San Diego.

Let me tell you little bit about me, and, hopefully, it will relate to some of your own life's goals. I started out as a 137-pound typical, skinny, skull-and-bones figured frame. It wasn't until a certain time in my life that I was motivated enough to begin transforming my body in such a way that I could proudly stand tall and say I have a 185-pound muscular body. The inspiration that I received during that process is exactly what I want to pass on to anyone I can.

It is my utmost goal to help others like my old self and those who want to change their body for the better, whether it be overweight or underweight. As an athlete from the time I was growing up and playing sports and basketball, to now, when I am eager to change people's lives, I want you to experience that same feeling I had during my transformation into, what I am proud to say, is the new Genesis today.

After spending some time training at a bigger gym, I wanted to reach as many people as I could. I was also getting requests from my network who could not make it to the gym where I trained. By starting Genesis

Fitness Training, I was able to train in homes, at a local studio and online as well. This gave me the opportunity to really help people. This also allowed me to learn so much about all types of different walks of life. I have had the honor to help hundreds of people, and I want to continue to reach more people by public speaking and books like this ☺. I have a passion to help others see what they cannot see in themselves.

I also want to give a 'shout out' to my right-hand woman, Alicia Agiler. She is the manager, the backbone and inspiration for our clients. Love you girl! We will continue this mission of empowering as many people as we can!

Genesis Read - "100% committed to changing lives "

BECOMING A TEAM

by Jim Reeves

I know this book is constructed with stories geared towards a fitness theme, but personal struggles are also present in high performance athletics, and I wanted to share a story I experienced over the last four years that I think you will connect with on a certain level.

I work as a sports performance coach for athletes in Mississauga, Ontario, a suburb of the largest Canadian city of Toronto. I work with high performance youth and professional athletes but, being from Canada, the number one passion I see in the athletes we work with is hockey. Every year, young athletes, parents, and their coaches consult with me to augment their on-ice game and add high performance training and personal development strategies to their hockey world. These athletes are driven, looking to move from the minor hockey system onto the next level - being drafted to the Ontario Hockey League (OHL) at sixteen years of age and/or committing to a scholarship offer at a university in Canada or the United States. These are the steps towards the possibility of having a professional career in the sport of hockey.

A lot of work goes into the success of these young athletes, and a lot of sacrifice too. Long hours in hockey rinks in the frozen grips of another chilly winter, travel tournaments as well as driving to and from practices and games most nights of the week. In their personal time, players are shooting pucks in their driveway, practicing their skating or stickhandling skills, working out or focusing on their food intake and sleep strategies in an effort to gain any slight advantage over the competition. And the competition is staggering.

I regularly discuss this topic with players I work with, and I try to illustrate for them what their chances of "making it" really are. When you critically look at the numbers, it's only about 5-6% of the total number of players in an age category that will play games at the next level in the year following. And there's no guarantee that these players will last, even if they make it that far. So, the pressure to gain any personal advantage is massive for many of these athletes and their families.

Unfortunately, the deck is stacked against most of the players. By the time players reach the Minor Midget year, at 15 years old, powerhouse teams have been in the works for years and the politics of youth sports is firmly entrenched. Basically, top teams recruit the best players possible and the best players are only looking to go to the best teams available. There's very little wiggle room on this movement, year over year.

It's a catch-22 situation. The middle and lower ranked teams have little ability to recruit highly talented players. Even if a coach of one of these weaker teams does a good job one year and helps some players develop in the previous season, these players are then recruited and leave to take a spot on a highly-ranked team. Then that coach is left trying to fill the player void again. It's a have or have-not scenario. The top teams cherry-pick the best talent, and the weaker teams are left to fill their roster from the remaining pool of players.

The ultimate problem with this scenario is that players are not usually drafted or recruited from most mid-pack or weaker teams. The scouts focus their time and scrutiny on the top teams only, players on lower ranked teams just simply miss out. And if you aren't scouted, as an individual player, your opportunities are really limited to move up the hockey ladder.

I worked with a team who was caught in this very scenario four years ago. The Brampton 45's, a 2001 birth year hockey team had just finished the previous 2012-13 season ranked #55 in the 63 team AAA division in the province of Ontario. In their geographical region, called the Ontario Minor Hockey Association (OMHA), Brampton had finished third to last in their 29-team league with a record of 16 wins, 40 losses and 8 ties. The team's coach, Randy Smith, spoke with me at length about his plan for the team, the accountability and personal development he wanted to achieve, and his willingness to forego short term success in the win column at the expense of teaching his players how to play a successful personal and team game.

For the next four years, the team trained at our facility every week. A core group of the players also attended our facility throughout the year on their own personal training programs, working out up to five sessions a week on their own throughout their spring and summer off-season.

The first two and a half years were tough. The improvement started slowly in the 2013-14 season, the team did not improve and finished with a record of 10-39-6 and a provincial ranking of 54th. Some of the initial gains and strengthening of the team were masked by the available talent and drive of players that Coach Smith could recruit. Not all of them had what it takes to be a winner at this level and, although the team made huge gains in their ability to play a more competitive brand of hockey, the improvements were modest overall.

The team steadily improved, finishing the 2014-15 season 16-30-4 and ranked #47 but the personal development that had shown in the players and the ability to play a more complete team game allowed Coach Smith to selectively recruit that year and bring in more stability and talent to the team's line-up. The following season, the team climbed over a major hurdle and suddenly, they were playing competitively with the best teams. Gone were the days of automatic losses against good teams. They were surprising everyone except those of us who saw the work they had put in so far. Both on and off the ice, the accountability and teaching continued, and the results began to show through.

The team improved to a 41-21-8 record in 2015-16 and jumped up to a provincial ranking of #22 heading into the playoffs. But Brampton wasn't finished there and with the taste of success, they wanted more. They seemed to peak at the right time of year. The team finished the playoffs winning a Bronze Medal in the OMHA playoff finals, knocking off several heavily favoured competitors and climbing an astounding 23 spots in the OMHA league standings in just three seasons.

Now, heading into the most important year of their minor hockey experience, Brampton was a contender. Through the first two months of the 2016-17 season, Brampton charged out of the gate and climbed to a provincial ranking of #5 after ten games, with an 8-1-1 record. The season continued to play out, and the players seemed to take on the persona of a top contender this year. I could see a personal confidence and swagger in each player that had not been there in previous years. Brampton continued to challenge the other top teams in both league and tournament play and entered the playoffs with a complete reversal of their won-loss record from only four years previous. They now had a record of 45-19-6!

In the 2017 playoffs, Brampton went undefeated and qualified for the season-ending play downs, a five-team tournament of the OMHA's regional playoff champs. In this tournament, Brampton continued their strong play, winning three of four games, and qualifying to play in the championship OMHA Gold Medal game. As they prepared for this final game, Coach Smith reflected on the "overnight" success that his team seemed to have. We spoke about how important the individual accountability from the coaching staff and myself to the players throughout the last four seasons had been in contributing to the team's success. They weren't a successful team that relied upon one or two superstars to win games. In fact, some scouts that I had spoken with had actually referred to the team as 'playing a strong team game' as the only reason for any success they had. But Brampton had done it. When no one would give them any credit, they had come out of nowhere and knocked off all the competition to gain their rightful spot in the OMHA's Gold Medal game during the most important year of their minor hockey experience.

The finals had Brampton facing off against the Whitby Wildcats, a team that was always strong and full of talent. Brampton would be in tough against this team, as the 2001 Wildcats had already been crowned OMHA Champions twice before. The championship game was a nail biter, with the teams tied 1-1 after the first period, tied 2-2 after two, and tied at 3-3 with less then 3 minutes to go in the final period. Then, a fluke play led to a pass deflecting off the skate of a player and past Brampton's surprised goaltender.

Brampton was down 4-3 and pressed hard in the final couple of minutes but ran out of time and, ultimately, lost the game to Whitby. Although they didn't win this game, Brampton had technically "Won" the Silver Medal, improving again on their Bronze Medal finish from the year before.

But the bigger victory was on a personal level for all these players. Going from a group of players who struggled so hard to try and keep up with other teams just four year before, they had risen from one of the weakest teams in the province to a team on par with so many of the best in their age group. On any given day, they now could win when challenged, no matter who they faced. And the thing is, there remained a core group of players from four years ago who were still with the team, and only two additions were made in recruiting players for this final season. Coach Smith had stuck by his core group of players through it all. So, the team, as a whole, had made this happen. This wasn't a recruiting success story at all.

Through their hard work, discipline, team effort and work ethic, the Brampton 45's did what no one except coach Smith and myself knew they could do. With their success on the ice, this Brampton team made sure that each of these players would be evaluated by scouts along with the other top level teams for the OHL draft and other opportunities to play hockey at higher levels. The players on this Brampton team had taken their dreams of success and acted upon them with a workman-like quality, tackling each workout and on-ice session with the intensity and focus necessary for them to make this climb.

Next up is the OHL Cup Tournament. Brampton has secured their spot in this prestigious year-end tournament of the top 20 Minor Midget teams from Ontario and the northern US. This is the tournament every young AAA player dreams of playing in during their minor midget year, displaying their talents in front of hundreds of OHL and NCAA scouts and just two weeks before the OHL draft. Anything can happen at these tournaments and I know the Brampton team has done the work over the past four seasons to put themselves in a great situation to succeed.

Each of those individual players has already succeeded in my eyes. By even being invited to play in the OHL Cup, they are playing at a level that was simply unimaginable even two years ago for them.

I'm looking forward to seeing how these young men do.

ABOUT JIM REEVES

Jim is a Certified Athletic Therapist, Registered Kinesiologist and Certified Strength & Conditioning Specialist with 19 years of experience working with youth and professional athletes.

Jim operates his own sports performance-training center called The Athlete's Zone in Mississauga, ON. The 8000sq.ft. facility is home for many amateur and professional athletes, specifically designed and outfitted to complement the advanced techniques and style of development today's high performance athlete demands.

Jim is the Strength & Conditioning Coach for the Mississauga Steelheads of the Ontario Hockey League, is also the head strength coach for the North Mississauga Soccer Club Rep Program as well as the off-season coach for many professional, amateur and NCAA athletes across a number of sports in the Greater Toronto Area.

Jim and his wife Leanna have four children: Evan, Kyle, Nicholas and Madison and live in Newmarket.

BRITTANY'S BREAKTHROUGH

by Wayne Salter

Growing up in Nashville, NC, Brittany did not think of herself any differently than any of the other kids. She played soccer, t-ball, and cheerleading, with Barbie dolls, had sleepovers and went to school. Her personality, her humor, her little girl wishes and desires were just like her friends. Like any other child, she grew up with hopes and dreams. But Brittany was not like "the other kids," at least as other people saw her. Brittany was overweight. She first realized it when kids began making fun of her size.

As the school years went by, the comments and ridicule increased. "I remember in 3rd grade when a girl told me that her thighs were smaller than mine. And when some kids would ask why I was fat." Incidents like this grew in frequency, and Brittany became more and more self-conscious about her appearance.

Then came high school, when self-image is being molded for a teenager. It is also a time when the sharp sting of a flippant comment can hurt the worst. Brittany painfully remembers comments like, "Guys would like you if you were skinnier," or They just don't make cute clothes for people your size."

In high school, she became "the fat friend.". She was taken advantage of by other girls, and by guys as well. "Guys, specifically, would show interest in me to allow them to become closer so girls in my circle of friends so they could date them." And girls would do the same to meet and hang out with the guys Brittany was friends with. Even though Brittany knew it, she did not care. She just wanted to fit in and be like everyone else.

Becoming more and more self-conscious and depressed, led her to over-eating. She began eating more and more between meals. She gorged on Chinese and fast food. She avoided mirrors. If she had to have her picture taken, she would try to hide her body behind something or someone else. She learned the tricks of taking selfies to make herself not look as overweight.

It was not until the college years that Brittany attempted to tackle the extra weight. Being in a sorority would make this easy, or so she thought. She joined in with friends on occasional workouts, usually centered on ab exercises, because that is, of course, where everybody wants to lose fat, right? The workouts with the sorority sisters were hit or miss at best, and eating better was not part of their plan. Many times after a workout, they would hang out at the local downtown eateries. Frustration with not losing weight only drove Brittany further into depression and toward more fast food.

In 2014, Brittany's friend, Morgan, was an exercise major. Morgan needed to do a project where she trained someone for 6 weeks. Of course, Brittany enthusiastically volunteered. She saw great results. She lost 12lbs and had more self-confidence with the weight loss. The guidance and accountability from a trainer really helped! Unfortunately, Morgan graduated and moved away. This left Brittany without the support she so desperately needed.

Brittany remembers, "The motivation needed to continue and the true desire to change my life was not there. I knew I needed to lose weight, but I did not WANT to."

In January 2015, Brittany decided to join a big box gym. It was loaded with treadmills, ellipticals and weight machines, and because she was surrounded by like-minded people, she felt that surely this would be the place she would see results. Not knowing what else to do, Brittany focused mainly on doing cardio for about an hour and occasionally venturing out to do a few machines. This approach saw little results and fizzled out.

In July 2015, Brittany took a trip to the theme park, Busch Gardens, in Virginia. She was excited to ride the popular ride, The Griffon, with a harrowing 90 degree drop straight down. After waiting in the long line, it was finally her turn to board the ride. With people rushing and scrambling to grab a seat, Brittany stepped onto the ride and backed up to her seat. After trying to squeeze in a few different ways, she could feel the stares of those around her. That's when she realized that she would not be able to fit in the seat. Highly embarrassed, she exited the other side. Feeling the eyes of the crowd on her, she knew that they knew. She tried justifying it on her "genetically wide" hips, but no matter the reason, this was an experience that she would always vividly remember.

After a trip to the mountains in February 2016, Brittany saw herself in a picture. Because she had naturally been avoiding cameras, she was shocked by how much weight she had gained. She decided to try working out again – this time, with her friend, Olivia. Their plan consisted of following workouts they found on Pinterest. Not following any particular plan and seeing little results, her momentum fizzled out again.

In April 2016, Brittany had a doctor's appointment. She could not remember the last time she had stepped on a scale. Not knowing how much she weighed, she guessed she was about 230 or 240. She was totally surprised and embarrassed when she saw the scale. It read a shocking 290 pounds!

After meeting with the doctor, she was informed of the gloomy news. She was pre-diabetic. She had threats of polycystic ovaries which could potentially dash her hopes of ever being able to bear a child. She also had cardiac issues that her doctor said was caused by her obesity. At the young age of 22, Brittany had potentially serious medical issues. This, of course, depressed her even more, but instead of trying to do anything about, Brittany just buried her stress in food.

A couple of weeks later, Brittany met her good friend, Lillian. She immediately noticed that Lillian had lost some weight and looked and acted happier. Lillian told her she recently joined an indoor boot camp, and she loved it. It was only a 30-minute class, was different every day, and it was a fun and caring atmosphere. She encouraged Brittany to come with her to try it out.

Brittany considered it, but thought it sounded intimidating. After a few weeks, her boyfriend encouraged her to just go try it once. So, eventually, she contacted Lillian and told her she was ready.

She was excited when she survived her first 30-minute session! She saw that it was, indeed, fun. Also, being in a group of people of all different fitness levels that were friendly and supportive made this seem very do-able. She returned for 2 more free visits. On the 3rd visit, the owner of the boot camp, Wayne, encouraged her to sign up for a 3-week trial period. After 3 weeks, Brittany was hooked. In that short time, she had lost about 8 pounds. She thought if she saw results like this in 3 weeks, what could she achieve in a year?

Lillian and Brittany made a decision that they would hold each other accountable with coming to boot camp and sharing what they ate. It was also at this time that her boyfriend of two years, James, took her on trip to Washington, DC for her birthday, and they got engaged.

With all of these events happening about the same time – the fateful doctors visit, seeing Lillian's transformation, and now, getting engaged - Brittany had the motivation she needed. She knew that this was a program she could stick with. Why? She did not have to worry about what exercises to do and it was only 30 minutes. She was also pleased to hear that Wayne supported eating a variety of clean and healthy foods – nothing too restrictive and no expensive fat burning pills or supplements - just plain old healthy food.

One of the suggestions Wayne gave her was to use a food tracking app. "Be honest with it. It won't do any good if you only put in the healthy stuff. Put in everything and make sure you use accurate amounts too. Don't worry about the calories. Let's focus on getting enough protein and fiber…"

Whatever Wayne suggested made sense, so it was easy to follow, at least most of it. There were some things that did not make sense at first, like the "not worrying about calories" part. She had always believed and been told that to lose weight you had to eat less. "That's not always true", Wayne said.

He also told her that she needed to aim for a steady blood sugar. This meant eating healthy snacks between meals aiming to never be hungry. Another suggestion was to eat more healthy fats. Some of these guidelines sounded counter-intuitive to Brittany, but she decided to go on faith.

Coming to boot camp consistently, Brittany saw progress on a weekly basis, and not just on the scales. She began to feel stronger. The workouts were always challenging, but she found herself using more weight and doing more reps, and her endurance was improving. She began having more energy during the day and sleeping better at night.

After a few weeks, Brittany realized she was happier on a daily basis. She felt more confident. Her clothes were fitting better and better and soon she was having to buy new clothes in a smaller size. "What a great problem to have," she thought!

Not only was she experiencing the change within and without, but others began noticing and complimenting her.

People would say, "You're looking thinner," or "You're looking really beautiful." She had never heard compliments like that before. Thinner? Really?

Her self-confidence sky-rocketed. Things that some people take for granted, were triumphs for her. She remembers when she was being able to do her first "real" burpee without having to do any modifications. "It was a huge deal to me," she says. These positive affirmations from friends and family were motivating her.

She knew that this was something she could stick with. She finally realized that being overweight was not her identity. It was something that she COULD control and change. She began to picture a life being a healthy weight and more fit. She was now on a mission! No longer would she sit and feel sorry for herself, trying to bury her pain in food!

By Thanksgiving, Brittany had lost a little over 40 pounds. She had already set her sights on losing 100 pounds in a year, but, with the holidays, comes delicious holiday treats. Brittany was afraid that the temptations of these foods were just going to be too much. Would she fall off the proverbial wagon and gain back weight she had lost??

It was just before Thanksgiving that Wayne introduced a program to help boot campers get through the holidays. It was a concept that sounded promising to Brittany because Wayne said they could still eat their favorite holiday foods!

"You just have to plan ahead. Some days you'll need to eat less, and some days more. Plan your high food intake days to be on days that you can indulge in the goodies and, if possible, get in a workout on those 'high' days too! Fluctuating your food intake like this should keep your metabolism going strong."

This sounded promising to Brittany and she breathed a sigh of relief. She made it through Christmas and still lost a couple of pounds! By the end of the year, she had hit the 50 pound mark.

Brittany soon discovered other goals that kept her motivated besides her physical transformation. One of the exercises they occasionally did in boot camp was dead hangs. In the beginning, she had to do the modification: stand on a box under the pull up bar and hang as much with your arms as you could, while standing on the box as little as possible.

In the beginning, Brittany felt like she was holding up more of herself with her legs than her arms. Each time, though, she would use her arms more and her legs less. After a couple of months she got to the point where she was only supporting herself on bent knees and her tip toes! In March 2017 Brittany was able to hold herself up by her arms only (no feet!) for a whole 30 seconds!

Wayne would occasionally touch base with Brittany – sometimes before or after a boot camp session, or by text. In February, he checked in. "How are you feeling? Still seeing progress? You getting enough protein? Are you eating enough??"

"Yes!" she texted back. "I feel like I'm eating all the time!"

As of this writing, Brittany has undergone quite the transformation. The scales currently register about a 67 pound weight loss. But it has been so much more than just a number on the scales. She says it is only the beginning.

"I want to lose a total of 100 pounds by July – that will be one year. I also want to help others who are feeling how I used feel. I want to be a voice of hope! I want to help them believe in themselves. I understand the pain that people are feeling, and I want to extend a helping hand!"

Brittany and Wayne want to hear from you. What is holding you back? What do you need to push yourself into making that decision? That decision that propels you into taking action!

Brittany wants to help and encourage YOU on your own journey. You can contact her, and continue to follow her, through her blog at: www.fitbritt17@blogspot.com.

ABOUT WAYNE SALTER

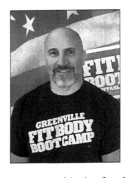

Wayne Salter is the owner of Fit Body Boot Camp in Greenville, NC. Owning a fitness facility where people come to get fit has been a dream of his for over 20 years. But it's been a long road.

"After serving in the Army (82nd Airborne Div.), I was faced with the reality that owning a gym would have to wait because of lack of money and lack of a plan.

After 9/11/2001, I decided to pursue becoming an ACE-Certified Personal Trainer. I loved helping people reach their weight loss and fitness goals! I was a full-time trainer in a box gym for over 5 years.

Then, instead of giving in to the desire to re-join the military, I decided to become a police officer. I continued to help people with their fitness goals "on the side" of my cop job, including fellow officers that I serve with, on our Emergency Response Team.

Even though I enjoyed the fulfilling and challenging job of being a police officer, there has always been that burning desire deep inside to own a fitness facility.

Taking out two different loans, I opened our boot camp in December, 2015. I juggled both the gym and being a cop. After a year, I went full time with the boot camp.

Helping people transform their lives on the outside as well as the inside has been even more rewarding than I imagined.

I feel very thankful and blessed and I'm excited about the future".

Wayne is also a certified Kettlebell instructor.

If you'd like to find out how Wayne can help you on your fitness journey, contact him at: fbbcGreenville@gmail.com

MAX STRENGTH

by Jeff Tomaszewski

When Debbie first heard of MaxStrength Fitness, she was experiencing severe joint pain in both of her knees at the age of 49. Her doctor told her that she would need both knees replaced but that she should wait until she was 50. When her boss told her about a fitness facility that took a very different approach to exercise, she was more than intrigued.

At MaxStrength Fitness, we take a very clinical approach to exercise. Our high-intensity, low-force protocol, performed in a clinically controlled environment (no mirrors, music or excessive socialization, not to mention keeping the temperature controlled at 67 degrees so you won't overheat and sweat), includes a total body workout in 20 minutes, twice a week. Workouts are brief and intense.

Debbie, like many others, found it hard to believe that you could get any results in only 20 minutes, twice a week. Little did Debbie know that her experience would be life changing.

She decided to give MaxStrength Fitness a try because she was desperate and could barely walk without excruciating pain. After training for a while, her newfound strength and function allowed her to travel across the country as President of the National Women in Construction. "I know without the strength I gained from MaxStrength," she said, "that I wouldn't have been able to travel as much as I did during that time."

Debbie's goal, in the beginning, was to prolong having her knees replaced. She was very successful, and put it off until after she was 52. By that time, she knew that she had gained a substantial amount of strength which would prepare her for her upcoming surgery. Debbie had a left total knee replacement in 2011, and the right in 2012. Her doctors and therapists were amazed at her recovery, which she attributes, primarily, to being very strong from her time at MaxStrength Fitness.

Although Debbie had lived many years in terrible physical pain, she did not realize how much emotional pain she was in. Every day was a struggle. She was often depressed and experienced pain levels of 12 out of 10. She gave up on the cardio she would do at work. The pain was so bad that she would go home and cry. Fast forward to 2014, which Debbie says was "the worst year of my life, and the best year as well."

When Debbie was in the hospital for her knee replacements, her husband of 20 years would barely come visit. He said he didn't like hospitals. In 2013, Debbie shifted her focus to trying to lose weight, but was unsuccessful due to depression. The next year, 2014, was to be the year that marked Debbie and her husband's 20th wedding anniversary. She really wanted to take control of her life and her marriage, so she asked her husband to escape on a getaway to the Bahamas, and he said, "No." For Debbie, this was the moment when she knew something was seriously wrong with her marriage.

In May of 2014, Debbie was traveling and presenting in Pittsburgh. She cut her trip short so she could be home to celebrate her 20th wedding anniversary with her husband. When she got home, she discovered that a bicycle that her mother had given her, along with a diamond bracelet, were missing. Debbie asked her husband "Where is my bike and my bracelet? They are missing."

He said, "I sold them."

215

When Debbie asked why he would do such a thing, her husband proceeded to verbally abuse her, and then he drew a gun from behind his back. He put it to her head and said, "I'm going to blow your brains out."

Debbie looked him dead in the eyes and shouted, "Do it! Just do it!" At that point, Debbie had given up all hope. She didn't care to live anymore. She no longer cared about herself or her life. She kept that incident to herself for 4 days until her boss noticed that she was acting very strange. When he inquired, Debbie revealed her horrific encounter with her husband. He instructed her to contact an attorney, and they would help her to leave her husband.

One of the hardest things was to tell all of her girlfriends. When she finally confided in them, her friends immediately handed her a house key and told her to get out immediately. She declined because she wanted to do it her way. For 2 weeks, she made a plan with her attorney, family and friends. On the day she left, she woke up and made her husband breakfast and dinner for the evening. When he left that morning, her friends came over with a list of everything she was taking and, within a couple of hours, she packed all she needed and left the life she had known for 20 years.

Debbie had gained back the weight she had lost by training with MaxStrength Fitness, but she was now more determined than ever to take control of her life and make it the best she could. She had a new fire to drive her every single day, and she wanted to live! She recommitted to her health and fitness goals and went back to training.

Now when she trains, she looks forward to her sessions because she knows that is a large piece to transforming her life and living the life of her dreams. She loves the atmosphere and team at MaxStrength Fitness. She said, "When I walk into the gym it feels like I'm with family, not just a trainer. They understand me, know my physical and emotional states and help me become the best version of me possible."

Debbie is putting herself first so that she can be healthy and fit and inspire others to live the life they desire. She says,

"I have a new appreciation for life, and I know that if I don't take care of my health and fitness first, then the rest of my life will suffer. Now if I get nervous or upset, rather than turning to food, I go for a walk. When I wake up in the morning, the first thing I do is check the weather to see if I can walk outside. The next thing I do is log into my MaxStrength Precision Nutrition program and read my daily lesson and practice my daily habit that leads to a healthy eating lifestyle. I look forward to my lessons. It tells me, every day, something to work on. I keep a journal. There's a lot of room for improvement, and I'm happy with that. I don't have the heaviness in my chest any more. The training and coaching at MaxStrength Fitness have helped me, now, live the life I've always wanted. I remember going to the beach with my girlfriends and having to sit along the shore as they walked up and down the beach, as I was not physically able to."

Recently, Debbie went to the beach with her new boyfriend and she put her feet in the sand and walked along the shore with no physical limitations. She is enjoying life, moment by moment, and has taken control of her health and fitness, and, more importantly, her life!

"MaxStrength has made me a stronger person, both physically and mentally," states Debbie. *"Because of that, I've helped several women get through similar situations of domestic abuse, and I'm able to share my story to inspire others that they, too, can change their lives. I wake up every day and look at the person in the mirror and want to be better. I want to live. That girl in 2014, who didn't care about herself, no longer exists. I want to live and be better than ever before. I want to be 96, like my grandmother, and enjoy my life and play with my nephews. I want to live! I want to one-day walk the Cleveland*

217

marathon! I want to go into a store and not worry about a price tag and not worry that they won't have my size. Now, I look forward to going to doctor appointments where I used to put them off. I've seen more of my family and friends than I did in 20 years married. I have a wonderful boyfriend who adores and respects me. Now, I don't let the small stuff worry me. I appreciate everything so much more. Life is great and MaxStrength Fitness has played a large part in it!"

If you find yourself struggling physically and think you don't have the time to transform your life like Debbie has, then perhaps MaxStrength Fitness is your solution. To learn how we help men and women just like you and Debbie transform their bodies, minds and souls in just minutes a week, go to www.maxstrengthfitness.com to learn more.

ABOUT JEFF TOMASZEWSKI

Jeff Tomaszewski is a graduate of Case Western Reserve University (Case) with a Bachelors of Arts in Psychology, a minor in Sports Medicine and a Masters degree in Exercise Physiology. He is a certified Athletic Trainer though the National Athletic Trainers Association and Certified Strength and Conditioning Specialist through the National Strength and Conditioning Association.

He began his career as a clinical Athletic Trainer for Ohio Physical Therapy and Sports Medicine and served as the Medical Coordinator for the National Youth Sports Program at Case. He went on to pursue a Master's degree and become the Assistant Athletic Trainer/Professor at Case in 2000. Shortly after obtaining his Master's degree he formed MaxStrength Fitness in May of 2007 in Westlake, Ohio, which has grown into Cleveland's premier personal training facility. A second facility was opened in May of 2017 in Willoughby, Ohio to help fulfill his life's mission of helping as many people as possible live a high quality of life into their golden years.

Along the way, Jeff obtained Professional Status as a Natural Drug-Free Bodybuilder solely using the methods and systems implemented at MaxStrength Fitness. Jeff is a graduate of the Goldman Sachs 10,000 Small Business Cohort 5 and is currently and active member in the

Entrepreneur Organization's Accelerator program and serves on the board.

Jeff and MaxStrength Fitness have been featured in Smart Business News, Mimi Vanderhaven, Cleveland Women's Journal, Boomer and Beyond, ESPN Radio, and has presented at countless seminars and business events. Jeff has also partnered with Prayers From Maria, a non-profit Children's Glioma Cancer Fondation. MaxStrength Fitness has committed to donate money for every training session they perform to help find a cure for childhood brain cancer.

Jeff is married to Jodi Tomaszewski, who is a partner at Dworken & Bernstein, LLP and has three beautiful daughters Emma, Chloe and Paige, and his beloved pet dog Maggie and cat, Sophie. When he is not busy transforming his client's lives through health and fitness Jeff enjoys spending time with his family splashing in the pool, taking walks and bike rides or any other adventure they can dream up. He also loves golf and any outdoor sports! Not to mention, rooting on the Browns, Cavs and Indians.

EVERYTHING IS POSSIBLE WHEN YOU BELIEVE

by Andreya Tornes

I met Mindy in an Anytime Fitness on a cold January day. She appeared to be a beautiful and vibrant young woman. As she started to tell me her quest for fitness I quickly realized that this was an unusual and special story. I also started to understand the angst and hint of sadness that I thought I saw in her eyes. Mindy proceeded to tell me that she was currently eating 500-600 calories daily, eating zero carbohydrates, and doing either running or her elliptical for and hour and a half each day. She had hired a popular diet weight loss company to help her with nutrition and this is how they had instructed her to eat. She had recently hired a male personal trainer to help her lose weight but the workout was so harsh that she could barely walk for days and even had a hard time standing up out of bed at all for days after It was extreme case of delayed onset muscle soreness, She needed to lose over 30 pounds and was currently at a weight loss plateau and no longer losing weight or getting the body definition and tone that she wanted.

Mindy's reason for wanting to get her body in body in shape was not just for vanity but rather special. She had a dream and a passion for singing. Mindy had been singing since she was a young girl. It was what she knew and loved. She was extremely talented and at the age of 22 was given the opportunity to sign with a popular record label and tour the country. At the time that is what she dreamed about but at the same time her Mother was diagnosed with a serious form of breast cancer. She loved her mother and had to turn down the opportunity to pursue her dreams. Shortly after that her mother passed away. It took Mindy down a dark road. Her mother and the opportunity to do what she loved were gone. She was in her 30s now and decided that it was her time she was going to pursue her love of singing again. She had been told by both her agent and multiple record labels that she didn't have the "Nashville look" that they were searching for. In most cases it is more about "beauty" rather then "talent" for success in any music industry. It was merely a fact in Mindy's mind that in order to open the door up to continue to pursue her dreams that she had to get in amazing shape.

AS we talked I could hardly believe what she was telling me. I knew as a trainer that eating that low of calories and doing that much cardio was sure to stave off muscle. This was unfortunately most women's go to for quick weight loss but in the end would not produce long term results. In fact it would only reduce the amount of progress that she would see hence the plateau she was in. Her metabolism was in the ground and I knew we needed to rebuild it.

As I planned out Mindy's program for long-term tone and weight loss I knew that it had to be employed in short term goals and steps. I needed to show her that she could lose weight and get the body she wanted with proper strength training, the right type of cardio (High Intensity Interval Training), and whole grain carbohydrates. The first few months in the gym I wanted to let her tell me what she was comfortable with, I did a full body strength training sessions. I wanted to show her that we did not need to crush the body and suffer to get to the goals that she wanted to attain. I wanted to gain her trust.

As time went on Mindy started to get more comfortable with heavier weights, and more intense cardio HIIT sessions. I even had her talked into eating carbohydrates in a carb cycle a few days a week. Her body was starting to respond. I was watching this beautiful soul transform. Her career as a vocalist was starting to take shape as well. She signed with a popular Nashville label. She then came into one of our sessions and said, "Do you think I could do a bikini competition?" I knew this was a big goal but I also knew Mindy. When she put her mind to something she was unstoppable. We agreed that this could be a good goal for her to work towards and possibly further her career in music.

Her journey to the fitness stage was amazing for her and I both. We had learned what worked for her body to achieve leanness and tone. She was working the program diligently. I could see her confidence skyrocketing. As an IFPA bodybuilder myself I knew this was no small task as there was a lot to learn with not only body results but presentation and posing but she was winning it with ease. She had learned how to balance out her life. It was like breathing for her. The pieces were falling together perfectly. The coordinator of the bikini show asked her is she would be willing to sing the national anthem at the start of the show—Wow we were pinching ourselves. At the same time record labels wanted to sign her. She was achieving her dreams. She had lost over 45 lbs. and her body looked amazing.

Her strength, faith, passion and success in her career and with her body were inspiring for me to see. I not only helped her to achieve her dreams but she motivated me on many levels to go after my own dreams and goals. She gave me many gifts along our 2 -year journey together one being a goal setting book. I can honestly say that this was the jump starter for me to start my own personal training studio. Yes, she was and is an inspiration.

Today Mindy maintains her weight loss and is more successful then ever. Her light and positivity soars on a daily basis. She continues to lift weights and compete in bikini competitions. One of the scriptures she keeps at the forefront of her mind when she tackles her goals is "Everything is possible for one who believes." She has recently completed a music video and is booked to sing live at the Grand Old Opry in June amongst other big names like Steve Martin and Kid Rock. Her success is unstoppable. I believe that her entire soul along with her body transformed and can see that anything she does in life will now find the success that she has proven to bring.

ABOUT ANDREYA TORNES

Owner of Tone 2 Day Personal Training Studio
ACE Certified Personal Trainer
Mindset Certified 1 & 2
B.S. Communications
Married for over 20 Years
Mom of 5 Boys

I started working out consistently at the YMCA in my 20s while taking my son to Tae Kwon Do Classes. I started out by using the elliptical and the bike. To my dismay at the time I was not seeing any body changes. I one day decided to try out a strength training class. After just 6 weeks of strength I noticed tone in my arms and abs. The scale actually went up in my case but my body looked better than ever! I decided that was my dream to get educated and work with people one on one as a trainer. I became passionate about the fun I was having and the success that I was seeing. I wanted to share it with everyone.

Working out became the light for me as I raised a large family experiencing busyness. The energy that I got from helping others find success and the connection that I experienced training others was the most rewarding in life.

I became an IFPA Pro Bodybuilder in 2013 and was nominated by Life Fitness as the "Top 10 trainer to watch in 2014" competition out of 137 countries worldwide. I started my own personal training studio in 2014 Tone 2 Day personal Training. In our first year, we quadrupled in size. I am currently authoring 2 books this year. I am passionate about helping others to love and find value in their selves. The first step in this process is usually taking care of their bodies and finding success here. This then gives them the confidence to move forward in other areas of their life where they may be stuck.

THE PURSUIT OF HAPPINESS

by Marty Velasco

Jen Sullivan has fought many battles throughout her life, the first of which started at the ripe age of 5. Her father was a chef and owned a butcher shop and grocery store and every occasion and function seemed to revolve around food. Late night eating, and nothing in the way of exercise, led to being overweight at a very early age.

Jen recalls always being teased and picked on as she was growing up, but she did not really notice that she was different from the other kids until her teen years. She dealt with her weight by working on everything else she felt she could control. Things like hair, makeup, nails, and clothes choices, all played a part in covering up the one thing that she could not control - her weight. There was not much support from her family when it came to trying to lose weight, and any sort of attempts to diet or get in shape were solo efforts.

Jen went to culinary school and, by the time she was 22, she had married a chef and shortly thereafter, began having children. She worked for the family catering business and was once again always surrounded by food. Her weight kept creeping up, to the point that she could lose 20-50 pounds and no one could tell. After a lifetime of dealing with negative comments related to her size and weight, Jen began to try dieting programs, like Weight Watchers, to help her lose weight. She was tired of the verbal abuse from the people around her and in her life.

Throughout her efforts to lose weight, she always attacked the problem from the food side of the equation, and never worked on doing any exercise to help build some muscle and speed up her metabolism. She felt that exercising was just too much work and with little kids running around, she felt she could control her food through journaling and that that would be the easiest way to lose the weight. This method yielded modest results, but it was not until she started running on the treadmill and working with weights that she started to see significant results. Through weight training and treadmill work, Jen was able to lose 70 pounds! And then, she had her third child and gained all of the weight back.

After the birth of her third child, Jen decided to leave the corporate world, start a daycare, and begin working from home. Jen thought that she could motivate herself to work-out and get in shape, but again, without a real plan or any guidance, she had no success on her own. She paid for entire gym memberships and never went, simply from a pure lack of motivation. She now found herself at a size 24 and a weight of 256 pounds. This was the heaviest she had ever been and she knew she had to do something about it.

"I was tired of being tired and unhappy every single day of my life, and I knew it was time to get serious," she said.

In the past, she had tried to lose weight to please other people, but now she knew she had to do this for herself! Jen was at a crossroads in many areas of her life, including her marriage and her career path, but her main priority was finding true happiness within herself.

It was at this time that a friend of hers introduced her to boot camp with us here at Fitness Edge in Lakewood, Ohio, and once she got started she never looked back.

"I was seeing huge change in just a few weeks of taking classes at Fitness Edge," she said, and she was motivated and inspired by other gym members who had had similar struggles with being overweight, and were now in the best shape of their lives!

Jen now feels and looks healthier, and has completely transformed her body and her life! From September of 2014 to May of 2016 she lost 110 pounds, dropping from 265 pounds to 155 pounds! Her body went through an incredible transformation, and she now realizes that being fit and healthy is a combination of not only proper diet, but proper exercise as well.

In March of 2016, because of her dramatic weight loss, she was motivated to go to the doctor and get a physical to see "where she was at" with regard to her health, now that she was in much better shape. That trip to the doctor changed her life. Her doctor did a full physical exam, and recommended she get a mammogram. She had the mammogram done and discovered that she had breast cancer. Women with her particular diagnosis often times have to go through multiple surgeries, and if they are obese, wait until they lose the weight to go through the entire treatment process. Jen was able to opt for a single procedure and be treated right away in May of 2016 because she was in good physical shape. Jen also attributes the discovery of her cancer to being in good shape because if she had not been, she would not have voluntarily gone to the doctor for a physical. If she had not gone, her cancer may not have been discovered until much later.

Needless to say, her perspective has changed quite a bit since going through cancer and losing all that weight. Jen says that being physically fit and active is a lifestyle for her. It is part of who she is and what she does, and not just simply a diet. She is much more in tune with her body and is now enjoying a new lease on life where she is happy and healthy. She is no longer living a life full of regrets.

The biggest take away that Jen shares with everyone who hears her story, is DO NOT WAIT. It kills her that she waited so long to take action and get control of her life. If you are in a position where you are not waking up happy and loving life every day, do something about it and TAKE ACTION. Find a gym, find a trainer, get a workout partner, do whatever you need to do to get the ball rolling and change your life!

ABOUT MARTY VELASCO

Marty Velasco founded Fitness Edge in 1998. He is an ACE certified personal trainer and sports performance coach through USA Weightlifting. He specializes in helping clients make a positive change in their life, no matter how old they are, or what shape they're currently in. His training style provides an experience that empowers, motivates, and inspires you to never give up!

Marty's entrepreneurial experience and success in small business has also led to coaching other small business owners in effective marketing and best-practices for successful business growth.

WONDER WOMAN'S SHADOW

by *Keith Wimsett*

I must admit, I am a bit of a comic book geek. When I was a kid, I read all kinds of comics: G.I. Joe, Superman, Hulk, you name it. But my favorite ones were the stories about average people becoming superheroes through fantastic circumstances. You know the ones. You have a guy or gal who are average, at best - not very popular, not very strong, and struggling with something internally. And then one day, BAM, something happens. They get bit by a genetically altered insect or hit by a bolt of lightning and the transformation from average to super begins.

Did I mention I love those stories?

Now, here I am years later and the owner of a personal training studio, Inspire Personal Fitness. I like to think that I am helping people go from average to above average on a daily basis. But average to superhero? That takes a special person and a special mix of just the right ingredients. I never, in all my years, thought I would see that, certainly not in my gym. But I have.

I remember when Kelly walked into my gym. I remember thinking that she was very passionate about health and fitness. She had a wonderful personality and was very likeable. I also remember the story of her struggle with body image:

"I used to be in a very dark place, for a very long time. Most of my late teens and twenties, actually, the, 'prime of one's life' so to speak, I was very depressed and deep in self-loathing. I was frustratingly overweight, despite a very healthy and athletic life. Granted, not nearly as overweight as the demons in my mind had convinced me I was, but, I had been struggling with my weight for quite some time. But there had been too many harsh comments in high school from mean boys that made me all too aware of how broad my shoulders were, how big my biceps and quads were, and just how disgusting they thought it was."

I began to exercise. A lot. Way too much. This was while in college, so I let my grades suffer because all that mattered was fitting in two, if not three workouts, every single day. Unfortunately, I also let the demon of eating disorders creep into my life. I became very good at making it look like I was eating, or that I had just eaten by the time my friends arrived at the dining hall. But, they knew, my parents knew, I wasn't fooling anyone. I was thin, sallow, dull, and unhealthy, and I had never been any of those things.

Insert silver lining: throughout all of this, People took notice of how much I knew about working out, and friends began to ask for help. Professors even asked to workout with me, and naturally, I obliged, and loved it. I had, without intending to, become very well versed in the world of health and fitness, so, I summoned all of my natural jubilant energy and happily helped. I saw friends that had been struggling with their weight and/or confidence completely transform right in front of me, because of me. Then, something else happened, I began to heal. Seeing the happy, healthy confidence my friends were gaining from feeling healthier, stronger, and fit, made me realize that I could make a difference, I could bring beauty from this shame.

As for myself, I had become healthy, too, both in mind and body. The temptation to get sucked back into eating disorders was gone, the constant comparing of

233

myself to unrealistic magazine covers had ceased, the desire to get thin and fit into a certain sized pair of jeans was replaced with the desire to become what I'm meant to be: STRONG! Instead of wanting to see the number on the scale go down, I focused on getting the weight I was lifting on the bar to go up. All of this came as a result of helping and healing others, from making a difference."

I still remember the first class she attended. It was our infamous (at least in my mind) "Gauntlet" workout. I warned her that this was a workout we did a few times a year as a way for members to gauge their progress and that she should pace herself.

It is a tough workout. Many of our long-term members could not finish it in the thirty-minute time cap. Kelly finished in twenty-seven minutes and said it was probably her favorite workout ever! From that moment, she was sold on Inspire, and I was sold on her.

Over the next few months, she continued to take on each class with an enthusiasm that was contagious. I noticed the other members working harder when she was there. I also noticed how she took the time to encourage them. Here she was, the newbie, encouraging (and inspiring) veteran members.

It wasn't long before I realized what I needed to do. One day, after class I approached her and asked if she had a minute to talk. I asked her how she was enjoying the gym. She said she loved it here and that it was the most supportive and fun gym she had ever been a part of. It was then that I asked her if she wanted a job. I could tell she wanted to say "yes," but I could also see that there was something holding her back (classic superhero story if you ask me).

"Eventually, Keith began dropping some pretty heavy hints that he would like me to stop being a member and start being a coach. He

234

saw the potential in me to continue building my own fitness and help coach others to reach the same goals. The thing is, I had been a coach and a trainer in the past, but it was at gyms that had almost ruined the job for me; very unfair wages, several unpaid hours, gyms full of college kids that were often inappropriate toward each other and toward me. I had had it. I was done. I wasn't going to waste my time and my dignity on coaching anymore. Although, I couldn't deny that this place was different, and even though I was well aware of that fact, the bitter ghosts of training jobs past still haunted my mind.

Nonetheless, Keith persisted, and, after several months of convincing and coaxing, I decided to give coaching a try again. I was extremely unhappy in the job I was working at that time, and again, I knew this gym was different. Initially, most members were either excited and/or confused, to see me transfer from being in the classes with them, to up front, directing them. The transition from member to coach went very smoothly, though, and felt extremely natural for everyone, it seemed. Then, things changed in my life. I woke up excited to go into work, I wasn't dreading the people I'd have to see throughout my day, but rather, looking forward to working with my new clients. My depression (I didn't even realize that I had been depressed) began to melt away, and I found a new purpose in each day: I was making people healthier, I was investing into their longevity, I was helping people reach their goals. It was then that I realized THIS is what being a personal trainer is all about. Inspire Personal Fitness made me realize dozens of things, with that point being amongst the most significant. I forgot that helping others to get healthy is what actually healed me.

That feeling of, "making a difference" all came flooding back to me the moment I started working as a coach at Inspire. I remembered why I initially fell in love with this work, on accident, and I haven't looked back since. The sheer number of deep friendships I have formed with people that have grown healthier and stronger is enough to fill my heart, day to day. Realistically, this work is truly a privilege! I get to take part in changing someone's habits for the better, I get to see them transform, bloom, and flourish, right before my eyes, and in return, I'm flourishing, too."

Remember I mentioned how it takes a special person and a special mix of the right ingredients? I did not know it at the time, but that is what this was.

Now here we are almost two years later. Her journey from a new member to a confident and inspiring coach is ongoing (every good superhero story is). But, watching her grow into an amazing trainer and person full of energy and compassion has been one of the best experiences of my life. And knowing that I, in some small way, helped her down that path has been incredible.

However, the most unexpected thing has been how her presence has changed me and my gym. The energy is higher, as are the expectations. She has now become the standard that I want my other coaches (including me) to aspire to. It is tough, at times, chasing the shadow of Wonder Woman, but I know that at the end of the day, she makes us all better.

When she first walked into my door I knew I wanted to help her. It is only now that I realize how much she has helped me.

ABOUT KEITH WIMSETT

Squatting as much as you can, as fast as you can? Nope. That does not happen at Inspire. There are gyms for that. Inspire isn't one of them.

Keith's mission is to help each person to get stronger, move better and feel awesome FOR THE LONG RUN: until their kids have kids and beyond.

In 1998 Keith became a certified kickboxing instructor and began teaching weekly classes at a local gym. Seeing the physical and mental changes happening to his students he decided he wanted to do more. After becoming a certified personal trainer through the American Council on Exercise in 2002, Keith quit his job as an art director and dedicated his life to fitness.

In 2006, Keith opened O3 Health And Fitness and then rebranded it to Inspire Personal Fitness in 2015. His vision was to create a supportive environment where members and coaches alike worked together as a team. Competition is fun, but Keith wanted to create an atmosphere that encourages each person to compete with the best version of themselves, not each other.

Keith is also committed to changing lives outside of his gym. That is why he has partnered with organizations such as Girls On The Run,

Brother Wolf Animal Rescue, St Joseph's Children's Hospital and Our Voice to raise thousands of dollars for charity and other causes.

Keith is a husband and also the father of two wonderful daughters, Ayla and Adira.

To connect with Keith directly about Inspire Personal Fitness or Local By Referral email him at: keith@inspirepersonalfitness.com.

AN ANGEL IN DISGUISE

by Fred Zoller

The phrase, "angel in disguise," has been said for hundreds of years, but it is always more amazing when it unfolds in your life. Sometimes it is chance, but all too often it comes during the most difficult of times. Well in this case, more than one angel was in disguise, and they have changed the course of a few lives.

I met Taylor in August of 2016 when she began training with us at LEAN Performance Academy. A few months earlier, I had spoken with her father about her, directly before he began his training and his journey with us. After 20 years in the fitness industry, I could always tell when a client's journey would be a difficult one, not only from the physical aspect, but emotional and spiritual as well. When I first saw Taylor, I could see the look of desperation on her face. I knew she needed help in a profound way.

Taylor and her family have struggled with weight issues for their entire lives. Food was a coping mechanism, but it tragically intensified during the two years she was enrolled in nursing school. The stress took its toll, and she was the heaviest she had ever been in her life. Taylor began to have multiple nervous breakdowns, especially in 2016 when she got the news that she had failed out of nursing school. She was devastated, knowing she spent two years of her life to find out nursing would not be her profession. Her solution was to turn to food. Now, between the weight gain and her perceived failure, life was taking a turn for the worse very quickly. She was constantly crying and depressed and needed to find help quickly.

After the semester ended, she decided to seek help regarding her weight and psychological state, and she made an appointment with her doctor. Taylor explained all that was going on in her life with her and the results of her testing quickly revealed that she was depressed, with severe anxiety. She was prescribed medication to help cope with the situation.

At this time, Taylor's dad was well into his training, and she decided that if he was doing it, she could, too. She didn't make the commitment right away because she lived over an hour away, and with school, it just did not seem feasible at the time. In April of 2016, she inquired about starting her training during the summer after school but was quickly asked, "Why wait?"

The next day, she messaged us and set up a meeting. She decided that NOW was a better time. Even though she was living a little less than an hour away from the gym, she made arrangements to drive there and back to finish her homework and be ready for school the next day. Her friends thought she was crazy for doing this, but she knew it was the way to get started living a healthier lifestyle. Even after one day of training, she recognized a change. She was happier.

When Taylor decided to make her transformation, all the changes together, coupled with stresses of life were very difficult. She was apprehensive about the gym, but knew it was a necessary step to a new life. There were many times when quitting looked like a viable option but her faith kept her going. As a few months went by, she began to fall in love with the process and see results both emotionally and physically.

At the beginning of her journey, Taylor was depressed, anxious, on medication and a size 20. That Taylor is long gone. Fast-forward only 8 months later, and now she is a size 14, very energetic and fit and off of all medications. She has grown tremendously as an individual through all the facility motivation. Today, Taylor faces her troubles head on instead of running to food or running away. Her life has changed, physically of course, but more importantly, mentally, emotionally and spiritually. God has placed her in a different career path to assist others like her who are in need of help. Her love for fitness and nutrition has allowed her to flourish in Health Promotion and Education. Although she prayed about whether it was the right decision to follow that path, it finally came to her. One day at the gym, during a training session of slamming balls, a sense of relief came over her and a weight was lifted off her shoulders. Health Promoting would be her new career path and "calling" in life.

This summer, beginning in June of 2017, Taylor will begin her internship at North Oaks Hospital as a health coach. She will be working with patients with chronic health problems, teaching them how to live a healthier lifestyle.

Failure is often thought of as the end. In Taylor's case, it was the beginning of a very beautiful and amazing transformation in every aspect of her life. I am confident that it will be for many others as well. It was her "angel in disguise." But as I mentioned earlier, it did not stop there. During this time, my wife and I developed a great relationship with Taylor and immediately saw all the amazing qualities in her. We were also in a very trying time looking for someone to help us with our 6 children in the busiest times of the day. Taylor fit right in with us and is now "Tay Tay," our sincerely beloved babysitter, nanny and friend. She inspires us on a daily basis with her passion, discipline and love for fitness, as well as being the best version of herself. She was our "angel in disguise." Our lives would not be complete without her, and our children love her. "For nothing will be impossible with God." Luke 1:37

ABOUT FRED ZOLLER

With over 400 active clients, Fred Zoller's LEAN Performance Academy is one of the largest and most successful performance-based fitness businesses in Slidell, LA.

Fred holds a B.S. degree in Kinesiology from SLU. He's earned numerous training certifications and has read and studied every ounce of material he could get his hands on related to health, fitness and business.

Fred's been a fitness coach and seminar leader since 1996 stemming from his career as a natural bodybuilder. He's worked with a wide variety of clients, from general population to several top-level athletes, State Champions, and professionals in a multitude of sports. A sought- after expert, Fred is invited to speak to a number of organizations each year about fitness, nutrition, motivation and business best practices. He's created a community within his facility and a proprietary training philosophy and methodology, which has been successful for over a decade.

Fred is committed to changing the lives of every single person he comes across on a daily basis. His efforts within the Slidell community have been responsible for raising thousands of dollars for charity and other causes. He's a devoted family man. His amazing wife, Nichole, six wonderful children and strong faith are his strongest 'reasons why' for being, giving and growing more.

To connect with Fred directly regarding LEAN Performance Academy, philanthropy, fund-raising, or community leadership, email is preferred, and yes, Fred answers every email personally in 24-48 hours or as soon as he can, at: fred@fredzoller.com

WANT TO BE A PUBLISHED AUTHOR?

Scriptor Publishing Group offers services including writing, publishing, marketing and consulting to take your book...

From Dream to Published!

Email us at
info@scriptorpublishinggroup.com
to get started!

67575268R00139

Made in the USA
Lexington, KY
16 September 2017